CLUSTER DEVELOPMENT

by
William H. Whyte

Foreword by
Laurance S. Rockefeller

AMERICAN CONSERVATION ASSOCIATION

30 ROCKEFELLER PLAZA, NEW YORK, N. Y. 10020

April 1964   Three Dollars a Copy

LIBRARY OF CONGRESS CATALOG CARD NUMBER 64-18592

Printed by Woodhaven Press Associates Corp., New York, N. Y.

Second Printing, July 1964

To the Memory of

CARL O. GUSTAFSON

one of the most effective friends conservation
and conservationists ever had

TABLE OF CONTENTS

FOREWORD

THIS is a report on a major new trend in housing. The American Conservation Association, which is publishing it, is a non-profit organization devoted to the preservation of nature and the enjoyment of its values by the public. Why, one might ask, should such an organization concern itself with development and housing problems?

Historically, what conservationists have sought is *non*-development and for them the developer and his bulldozers have seemed the natural foe. There are many good reasons for this attitude, certainly, and those who have been working to save our open spaces would not have accomplished much if they had not had this fighting spirit.

The time has come, however, for conservationists to take a much more positive interest in development — not just for the threat that it poses, but for the potentials that it holds. It is going to take place; and on a larger scale than ever before. But what will be its character? The answer to this question is critical to the whole problem of preserving the influence of the outdoors in American life.

Let me cite two of the major findings of the Outdoor Recreation Resources Review Commission. The first was that the crux of the outdoor recreation problem is in our urban areas. Here is where the land is the hardest to come by, and here is where the bulk of our population lives, and the concentration promises to become greater in the future. Far away parks make a great contribution, but the basic need for outdoor recreation in the metropolitan areas cannot be met somewhere else.

The second finding was that the use of private land is just as critical as the acquisition of public land. More parks are necessary, but they are only part of the answer. The most important recreation of all is the kind that people find in their everyday lives. What kind of subdivisions will the next generation live in? Will there be any woods or streams left for the children to experience? Will there be paths to cycle? Or, will it all be smothered in concrete? We are talking then about an *environment*. Thus our challenge: can we shape future growth so that the outdoors is an integral part of it?

Suburban development has been squandering the very resources that people have moved out from the city to seek. In a land wasting pattern that has used ten acres to do the work of one, houses on equal space lots have been spattered all over the landscape and the streams and the woods and hills have been ruthlessly obliterated.

Now a change is in the air. By applying the cluster principle, developers can put up the same number of houses but on a portion of the tract, with the bulk of the land left for open space and recreation. The promise is twofold; not only can the individual subdivisions themselves be far better places to live in; the shift to this pattern opens up tremendous opportunities for local governments to join the separate open spaces into a network that will weave the outdoors into the very heart of the metropolitan areas.

The crucial testing period is now at hand and the lessons are beginning to emerge. Few people are better qualified to pull them together than William H. Whyte. Mr. Whyte drafted the ORRRC study report on Open Space Action and has been one of the prime movers in the recent wave of open space legislation.

Rather than a definitive study after the fact, the aim was a firsthand report in time to help people shape the movement. Mr. Whyte and research associate Hildegard Ellerkmann began the study in May 1963, and over the next ten months they looked at cluster development from every possible viewpoint: in addition to checking scores of developments (and taking the pictures for this report), they talked with site planners, architects, engineers, civic officials, and followed up several revealing local controversies.

Whether the cluster principle fulfills its potentials will depend a great deal on the efforts of builders and architects. It will also depend on the influence exerted by planners, officials, and most important of all, the citizens. We hope this report will be helpful to them.

LAURANCE S. ROCKEFELLER

Village Green, Hillsborough, New Jersey.

Chapter I

INTRODUCTION

CLUSTER is on the verge of becoming the dominant pattern of new residential development, and probably for many years to come.

It is a counter revolutionary movement that is taking place. The cluster idea is ancient; what it calls for, simply, is grouping the houses more tightly together and using the land thus saved for common greens and squares. It is the principle of the early New England town; it is the principle of the medieval village, it is, in fact, the basic principle of community design since we first started building several millenia ago.

The revolution took place here, and quite recently. Fifty years ago we clustered housing without thinking much about it. For all the nostalgic image of the American homestead, most Americans lived quite close to each other, in towns and cities, and many of the best people lived in row houses. But then in the twenties the expansion of suburbia began gathering force, and what is known as the American's historic yearning for a home in the country was soon to be established.

By the fifties it was official. A growing urban population had now turned the move to suburbia into a great surge. This had the effect of under-cutting the reason for the move, for the countryside was always vanishing over the next hill, but the momentum was unstoppable. The detached house on a lot of one's own seemed to have become the norm of middle class aspiration.

There was no alternative, or so it seemed. With few exceptions the new subdivisions homogenized the land with lots strung out as far apart as income or pride could enforce. The design was embedded in countless local ordinances, in the lending requirements of the FHA and mortgage institutions, and perhaps more important, in the widespread conviction that Americans would accept no other design.

"Garden city" advocates had tried to prove otherwise, and through the efforts of Clarence Stein and others several model communities had been built on the cluster principle. There was Radburn in the late twenties, the Greenbelt towns of the early New Deal and in the late thirties Baldwin Hills in Los Angeles. Some of the Utopian expectations with which these experiments were freighted were never born out, but as individual communities they were, and still are, quite successful. But they remained outside the main stream. Some of their features were copied, such as the super block and the cul-de-sac, but the basic cluster principle was not. Few developers even bothered to go look.

BY the late fifties, however, the conventional pattern had been pushed close to the breaking point. No matter how far out developers pushed, land prices kept soaring ahead of them. Thus, as they moved further away from the center of their market, they found the cost of the land and of improving it was taking up a sharply increasing portion of the final housing costs. If developers were not to price themselves out of the mass market something had to give.

One solution would be to squeeze more houses onto the tract. But communities wouldn't allow this; indeed, they were more zealous than ever in using large lot zoning to keep down the number of newcomers they would have to school and service. For the developer the only practical solution would be to concentrate the allowable number of houses on the most buildable part of the tract and leave the rest open. The Urban Land Institute, the National Association of Home Biulders, and the leading housing journals commenced an impressive educational campaign on this concept.

Sprawl had been hurting the public most of all, and the fact was at last becoming quite visible. Large lot zoning was not keeping the subdivisions in check; it was making them chew up more and more of the landscape. This not only looked like hell, it was proving costly for the community to service. And what would happen when the next wave hit?

The Regional Plan Association has made such an estimate for the New York metropolitan region. By 1985 there should be an additional six and a half million people to house; on the remaining vacant land, however, the average lot size is now up to 2/3 of an acre, and if the pattern persists there could only be one result. The Association, which fervently hopes it never comes to pass, calls it "spread city" — "not a true city because it lacks centers, nor a suburb because it is not a satellite of any city, nor is it truly rural because it is loosely covered with houses and urban facilities."

In every metropolitan area the warning has been sounded. The mathematics have become inexorable; with just so much land and many more people we simply cannot continue to waste land the way we have been. If there is to be any environment worth living in, there must be a much more efficient use of the land. This calls for many approaches but the essence is the cluster idea, on the regional as well as the community scale, and with increasing urgency this point has been expounded in hundreds of local meetings.

CITIZENS have been interested, but cautious. Why be the guinea pigs? If we approved cluster wouldn't the jerry-builders come swarming in? How do you solve the problem of who takes care of the open space? That's a fine plan but did it ever get built? If this is such a hot idea, why haven't more communities tried it? Citizens want to be shown.

Now they can be. Many of the projects which were initiated three or four years ago have finally broken through the last crust of resistance. A few have been up for some time, a fair number have been completed and are shaking down, and an impressive number are now getting the final approval and are ready for the land grading phase. There has been a pick-up in the number of communities which have adopted ordinances to permit cluster development, and the increase could soon be geometric.

What are the chief denominators? We must first define terms — but not too finely. Cluster goes under many different names — density zoning, planned unit development, environmental planning — but it is the basic approach that concerns us. Rather than attempt a highly specific definition, let us think of a range. At one end we have the conventional subdivision in which there is no common open space. At the other end we have the cluster development of high density, siting towers or town houses around small common greens.

What is significant is not the exact degree of clustering. Lot sizes, after all, are relative, and what in one area would constitute high density clusters — one-half acre plots around a green, for example, in a four acre

zone — would in a more urban area seem anything but cluster. What is significant is the direction. There is a definite shift towards the cluster end of the scale, and this shift may presage a later move to higher net densities for all kinds of developments.

This does not mean that paradise is imminent. Nor does it mean that large lots and detached houses are on their way out, or that they should be. There is a place for each, and for the maligned rancher too. What we are really talking about is a more effective land use, and it is the new range of choice cluster provides that opens up the great opportunities.

They could be well seized, or they could be abused; at this stage the cluster movement is still highly malleable. That is the reason for this report. It is an effort to bring together what has been learned so far; to see which approaches are working out well, and which are not. The initial chapters concentrate on the major legal and economic factors. The middle chapters take up the specific cluster developments. In the concluding chapters we set down what we believe are the major lessons. In the Appendix is a tabulation of data for a cross section of 46 developments, and as a help to civic officials and citizen groups a selection of model ordinances, articles of incorporation for homeowners associations and deed forms are provided.

Here is a brief summary of the basic findings.

The verdict of the market place is yes. The sales data we have gathered have to be interpreted with care; every development is something of a special case and in any event sales figures have to be judged in relation to the local market. Nevertheless, one fact is becoming evident; in most cases cluster developments have been outselling conventional developments of the same price range.

It doesn't follow from this that people buy because of the cluster principle; other factors, most notably the house itself, may be more compelling. But one reason it is difficult to sort out cause and effect is that these factors tend to have an underlying unity in most cluster developments.

Those developers who have the imagination to try a new approach are most likely to be the developers with the best eye for house design. Cluster developments, as a consequence, tend to be better developments than the competition in a host of details as well as in overall concept. What weighting do buyers give the common green? The walkways? The swim club? Even they don't know. But they are buying and this is the key fact.

People like to live in cluster developments. Talks with homeowners indicate that while they may be quite unaware that there's anything particularly unusual about their subdivision, they show a high degree of satisfaction with it. Similarly, while the cluster element may not have been the motivating factor, it is one that they come to appreciate. When they were shopping their questions were primarily about the house itself, schools, nearby transportation and such. Once they become owners, however, the usefulness and amenity of the open space layout becomes more important and in talking to other people about the community they are likely to give it some emphasis.

Interestingly, there is often something of a time lag problem. People have to know how to use open space to appreciate it. Where the people have come from the central city, the kind of open spaces — such as stream, valleys and woods, for example — so familiar to country people can seem a downright menace, and mothers forbid their children to go near them. It will be interesting to see how the new generations respond.

The "town house" development is catching on fast. In most cases the town house is a row house that is not in town at all and is often extremely expensive. One could deduce that it's all wrong for the market, suburbia most of all. Add a Williamsburg facade, such touches as old fashioned gas street lamps, group them around common greens, and the result is a sales package that may turn out to be the "revolutionary" new concept of the next decade.

Some of the most successful of such developments have been in the upper brackets; Dudley Square in Shreveport, Louisiana, with its $40,000 houses, is a notable example. While town house developments do seem to have a certain tastemaker appeal the market success has been equally strong at the other end of the range, and it is in this bracket that developers are now sensing a bandwagon. In the Los Angeles area, the success of one town house development has been so great that developers all over the area have been junking conventional plans and have virtually swamped the local FHA office with applications for town house units.

There is a growing emphasis on recreation as a core element. Recreation facilities have worked well for many conventional developments and golf course subdivisions date back to the twenties. Such facilities are virtually called for, however, by a cluster layout. Some of the new cluster developments include golf courses, bridle trails, tennis courts and such, and several of the largest make recreation so integral a feature that they could be called "recreational communities." These feature a series of villages, each centered around a special recreational activity — swimming in one, for example; riding in another.

While facilities are much less elaborate in the smaller developments, as a minimum almost all include swim clubs and children's playgrounds. The day is close at hand, indeed, when a developer will have to provide them if he is to compete.

The basic procedures for common open space ownership and maintenance are working well. There are three basic methods. One, favored in New Jersey, is to deed the space to the local government. This seems the simplest course but for reasons which this report will detail later, it may prove the least effective. The second method is to set up a special governmental district, the boundaries of which coincide with that of the development, and deed the land to the district. Such districts are empowered to levy assessments on the residents for maintenance and development of the open space. The third is basically the same except that the vehicle is a non-profit corporation consisting of the homeowners.

There has been considerable experience with such associations, and as a study of them by the Urban Land Institute indicates, they have worked quite well. Key requirements: they should be set up at the very beginning; membership should be mandatory for all homeowners; there should be provision for assessments to cover costs, and for adjusting the assessments to meet new conditions.

WHAT problems remain? It may seem premature to worry about the disadvantages of success, but several warnings are in order. Because the developers who are pioneering cluster tend to be among the best, the overall standards tend to be well above average. But this is likely to be temporary; and the defects that are already apparent could well be magnified as the idea is taken up by more and more developers.

Cluster could be frozen into a format as stereotyped as the conventional layout it is replacing. The enthusiasm with which Los Angeles builders are hopping on the town house bandwagon may be a foretaste of what is yet to come: the externals of the best selling developments are likely to be repeated time and time again, whatever the site, the latitude, or the character of the area. If one had to guess the specifications of the all-

American development five years from now, they would probably run something like this: two-story row houses, Georgetown facade spiced up with West Coast Cinderella; the first floor featuring an open kitchen leading to living room, in turn opening out through sliding glass doors onto a patio twenty feet square, with a fence eight feet high, the gate opening out onto a common area roughly 100 feet across to the next row of houses, a play yard at one end with swings and abstract forms—the whole garlanded with gas street lamps.

There is nothing inherently wrong with this layout, save for those gas lamps, and some cluster developments that come close to these specifications are excellent ones. But what about the copies? Imitation has a way of missing the quality of the prototype, and as the copies go up the uniformity could be appalling.

Cluster development calls for a fresh approach to house design. In the outlying areas there can be clustering with relatively large lots and here the conventional detached house can work well. As lot sizes get smaller, however, there comes a point where the conventional design doesn't quite work. Windows on the side, for example, tend to lose their function. There's nothing to see except the neighbor's windows, and the vestigial strip of yard becomes a positive disadvantage.

More important, the relationship of one house's design to another becomes much more critical. In a conventional large lot subdivision with, say, five basic models, there may be enough space that a split level, barn red colonial can be sited next to a rancher without visual clash, and even a few Hansel and Gretels won't foul things up too badly. Bring the disparate elements close together, however, and what strikes the eye is chaos.

There is too much hack site planning. Cluster offers unparalleled advantages for imaginative use of topography — the use of trees as focal points, the use of rock formations, and overburden from grading operations. But there is far too little exploitation of these advantages.

In researching developments for this report one of the most disconcerting tasks was finding out who did the basic site plan. In some cases, evidently, no one did; in others, it started on the back of an envelope and then was handed over to a civil engineer to fill in. For the best developments trained site planners were used but in too many of these cases they were brought in only after the first plans proved unworkable. Developers would save money if they started with them in the first place.

There should be more experimentation with uses of open space—in particular, the relationship between private and common spaces. There is a lot of a dogma about how people should use open spaces, but remarkably little attention paid as to how people actually do use them. Formal play areas are an example: children seem to play almost anywhere else.

Cluster should not be used as a device to achieve unreasonable densities. Standardization would be bad enough; worse yet would be both standardization and compression. What appeals most to many developers, let us remember, is the cluster, not the open space: the doughnut and not the hole. Clustering can achieve higher densities and a more pleasant environment at the same time. But somewhere along the line the two part company.

There is a fine line between a comfortable sense of enclosure and being cramped, and some developments have pushed compression to the point of claustrophobia. In recognizing the effectiveness of a small open space it is easy to forget that the effectiveness is possible because the development has borrowed space from surrounding areas. Take away the larger areas and the smaller open spaces have a far different feeling.

Communities should not use cluster as a cut-rate substitute for buying park land. Just as developers should not make too much of a good thing of cluster, neither should communities. A number have been trying very hard, most notably in New Jersey. As part of the bargain for approving cluster developments, they are requiring that common open spaces be deeded outright to the town. It seems to be working well enough. The courts have indicated approval, the developers have not raised a fuss, and the towns have been getting a great deal of land without having to pay a cent.

But it is a bad precedent. To make municipal ownership an invariable condition is to undercut the basic rationale of cluster. It is the homeowners who are really paying for the common land, and they should be able to enjoy it.

This does not mean that dedication to the community is necessarily against their interests; in many cases, it is the best way for all concerned to handle the common area, in full or in part. But in many other cases it is not, and dedication to a homeowners association would be preferable. The community should demand guarantees that the open space remain open; it should decide the precise form of ownership, however, on the basis of the particular case. Thus to our final point.

The great promise of cluster is in the exciting opportunities there are for linking spaces together. For the community it is the connective quality of cluster open space that is most important and a relatively small part of the open space may be the link that ties many more acres together. The key is to anticipate cluster development and to lay down in advance the skeleton of an open space network that would unite the open spaces of one cluster development with the open spaces of others — and with the school and park sites of the community. It can be done; Philadelphia has demonstrated this.

The potential of cluster is great and that is what makes this particular point in time so tantalizing. The concept is not frozen yet. Eventually, the cluster concept may become codified and imbedded in various legislative and administrative regulations, much as the once new "superblock" pattern became virtually dictated by law. But not quite yet.

Cluster is still in the formative period. The very fact that cluster can mean so many different things may make definition difficult, but it does provide a rich field of experimentation. We have a chance to see which approaches are not proving fruitful, and what new ones ought to be tried. The time ahead is the critical one. Several years from now decisions will have been made that will probably set the pattern of American residential development for a long time to come. But the decisions are still ours to make.

Chapter II

THE ECONOMICS OF CLUSTER

Good aesthetics, it is said, make good economics. Cluster development, as this chapter will outline, is one instance where the thought is demonstrably true. Whether considered from the community's interest or the developer's or the homeowner's, the factors that make cluster developments look better are the same factors that make them more economical.

Until recently, the economic case had to be somewhat hypothetical. Most presentations would be based on a detailed comparison of the cost of putting up a conventional subdivision on a given tract of land and the cost of the cluster alternative. Since rules of thumb for costs are fairly standard—so many dollars per lineal foot of curbing, and the like—the comparisons could be realistic. Invariably, they favored cluster.

On aesthetics the comparisons favored cluster even more. Here imagination would be displayed, often very enthusiastically, and what with sketches of children gamboling on greenswards, outdoor cafes with striped umbrellas, and such, the vision held up approached idyllic proportions.

But the basic case is a strong one and it has been well presented. The National Association of Home Builders put together a travelling road show which has been shown to builders across the U.S. The FHA has been energetic in missionary work; it has been revising its regulations to encourage the new approach and as an invitation to builders recently published "Planned Unit Development With a Homes Association" (available at 50¢ a copy from the U.S. Government Printing Office, Washington, D.C.)

City and county planning agencies have also been assiduous, and over the past few years they have been putting out some notable why-don't-we-try-this presentations of the cluster idea. One of the best, shown at right, is that prepared by Karl Belser and his associates on the planning commission of Santa Clara County, California. It was used to good effect by planners and builders all over the country (eventually, Belser is happy to note, in Santa Clara County too).

Now the case need no longer be hypothetical; enough cluster developments are actually on the ground to afford first hand tests. One of the most significant is Village Green in Hillsborough, New Jersey. It is significant because there is nothing particularly unusual about it. Some of the very large developments may make a more striking case economically, but they tend to be complicated by a number of special factors. Village Green is characteristic of the kind of problems faced by the great bulk of builders.

Hillsborough is a semi-rural community whose 8,000 people want it to stay semi-rural. In 1958 the town had decided to raise the bars. With New York forty miles away and new highways going up, a mass invasion by developers seemed imminent, and to forestall this the town changed its zoning from a half acre to one acre lots. For a while this seemed to work.

In 1960 real estate man Sidney Halpern acquired a 79 acre tract and proceeded to plat it for one acre lots. Fortuitously the county planner, William Roach, was a member of the Hillsborough planning board, and he was keen on cluster. One afternoon he sat down with Halpern and sketched out on a piece of paper how a cluster plan would be a better proposition for Halpern than his conventional one. Roach's idea was to group the houses in three clusters on 35 acres and leave the remaining 40 acres open.

Halpern and his associate, Seymour Tuschak, liked the idea. So did the town planning board. It retained planner Robert Catlin to make zoning and designing recommendations. In 1961 the board unanimously approved a cluster zoning ordinance and subsequently approved the Village Green plan.

Builder Melvin Konwiser, who bought the package from Halpern, started off with a good edge on the competition. He could not only put up more houses, he could concentrate them on the prime sites. Under the conventional plan, he would have been forced by the topography to put up only 69 houses, and many of them would have to have been placed on less desirable portions of the periphery—land abutting the railroad tracks,

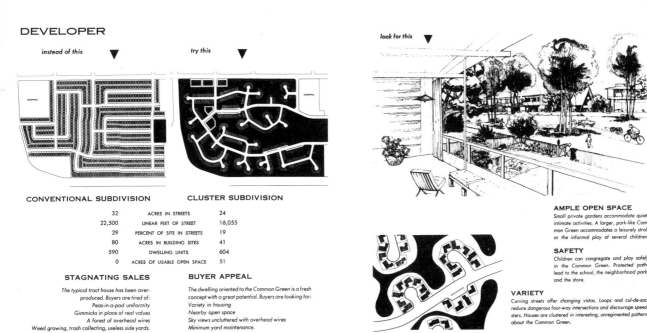

CONVENTIONAL SUBDIVISION   **CLUSTER SUBDIVISION**

CONVENTIONAL SUBDIVISION		CLUSTER SUBDIVISION
32	ACRES IN STREETS	24
22,500	LINEAR FEET OF STREET	16,055
29	PERCENT OF SITE IN STREETS	19
80	ACRES IN BUILDING SITES	41
590	DWELLING UNITS	604
0	ACRES OF USABLE OPEN SPACE	51

STAGNATING SALES

The typical tract house has been over-produced. Buyers are tired of:
Peas-in-a-pod uniformity
Gimmicks in place of real values
A forest of overhead wires
Weed growing, trash collecting, useless side yards.

BUYER APPEAL

The dwelling oriented to the Common Green is a fresh concept with a great potential. Buyers are looking for:
Variety in housing
Nearby open space
Sky views uncluttered with overhead wires
Minimum yard maintenance.

AMPLE OPEN SPACE

Small private gardens accommodate quiet, intimate activities. A larger, park-like Common Green accommodates a leisurely stroll or the informal play of several children.

SAFETY

Children can congregate and play safely in the Common Green. Protected paths lead to the school, the neighborhood park, and the store.

VARIETY

Curving streets offer changing vistas. Loops and cul-de-sacs reduce dangerous four-way intersections and discourage speedsters. Houses are clustered in interesting, unregimented patterns about the Common Green.

Excerpts from "The Common Green" brochure, fomented by Santa Clara County planners in 1961.

a highway, an industrial zone, and low cost homes of a neighboring township. Under the cluster plan, he was able to gain three more house sites. All of the houses, furthermore, were placed on the choicest part of the tract and the outermost of them, instead of being out the peripheral land, were bordered by the common open space.

Another saving was in water and sewerage. In the conventional plan Konwiser would have had to put in septic tanks and dig wells; because the tighter grouping of the cluster plan allowed shorter pipe runs, he would be able to tie them in with the water and sewerage facilities of adjoining Manville borough. Land development costs, estimated at $6,500 per lot for the conventional plan, were shaved to $5,500. There was less roadway and less grading. The trees, including a fine stand of hardwood, didn't have to be sawn away.

As he began to build the development, Konwiser discovered there were additional savings. He built the development a cluster at a time, and in doing so found he was able to concentrate all his materials and equipment in one place with a considerable savings in man hours and convenience. As soon as one cluster was finished he moved everything to the next cluster site.

The first cluster was ready for occupancy in the middle of October 1962; a month later it was fully occupied. The second cluster was opened up in December, the third in March. While there is no precise way of measuring the time savings, the speed of construction cut down Konwiser's overhead by a considerable

margin and got him off to an earlier start on sales.

The inevitable extras cut somewhat into the savings of cluster: Konwiser installed a drinking fountain, water lines, a baseball diamond, two bus stop shelters. He could well afford to. The houses outsold the competition—indeed, they knocked the bottom out of the market in the area for some time.

There was to be an interesting contretemps, but it didn't come about because of any defect in Village Green. The trouble was the opposite. As a later chapter will relate, Village Green was *too* economic.

IN establishing the economic case for cluster, it is the community aspect that is the crux of the matter. If anything, the benefits of cluster are even stronger for the community than for the developer but though this may seem self-evident to planners and developers it is by no means evident to local officials and the general citizenry. Nor is it self-evident to municipal engineers. They are a conservative group, and are naturally suspicious of innovations, especially those that seem to call for watering down accepted civic standards for construction.

Technical objections to cluster, we must note, are often more a rationalization for resisting cluster than the reason. The amenity appeal is what will sell cluster and as time goes on and there are more such developments to see, the technical objections will dwindle. It is important, however, to compress that time. Over

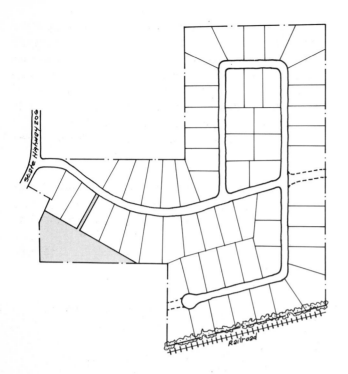

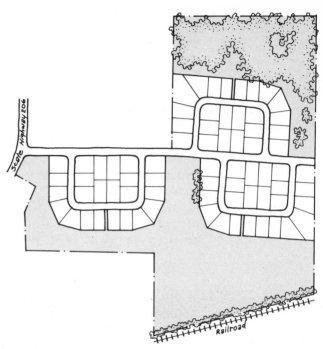

Village Green: original subdivision plan.

The cluster plan finally adopted.

the next year or so there are going to be bruising debates in hundreds of communities over cluster and the more fully the economic case is presented the less wear and tear for all concerned.

Probably the best way to start is with the least attractive factor: sewage. Under conventional development communities are faced with somewhat of a dilemma. If the community sewers an area, it virtually decrees that the area will be developed, and if large lot zoning is the rule, a prodigious amount of pipe will have to be laid. On the other hand, if it does not sewer an area, the subdivisions will be mostly of the septic tank variety and the large fields necessary can further accentuate the sprawl pattern. In either event, developers will do much of the installation; the extra cost, however, inevitably falls on the public.

A detailed exposition of this point has been made by the planners of Fairfax County, Virginia, in a recently published study, Suburban Cluster Vs. Urban Sprawl (Fairfax County Planning Division, Courthouse, Fairfax, Va. $1.50). They have particular reason to be concerned. The county is a near classic example of a rural area being rapidly urbanized, and there are only a few years left before the pattern of development for the western part will be set.

To demonstrate the savings of cluster over conventional development, the planners have put particular emphasis on sanitary sewers. Under present policy, they

argue, the county designs sanitary sewers to accommodate an average of 10 persons per acre or more. The ultimate extension of this policy, the planners argue, would be to homogenize development all over the place where, preferably, there should be a mixture — high density developments in some areas, but many large stretches left in open space or relatively low density development. The installation of a sewer system along conventional lines, however, makes hash of such plans. Where the sewers go development goes.

Should the sanitary sewers rule the development for the county, the planners ask, or should it be adapted to a comprehensive land use plan? Which would be more economical?

Taking one watershed as an example, the planners hypothesize three courses as a base for cost comparisons. Common to all three is the same assumed population, 110,000 persons. The first would be a sanitary sewer system designed to meet current specifications. This would be a network poking up into all the valleys and draws and would service pretty much the whole land area. It would cost an estimated $7,500,000 or $68 per capita.

The second approach is a "controlled access" system. This would total as many feet as the conventional, but some of the trunks would be smaller in diameter. Cost of the system would be $60 per capita.

What the planners clearly prefer is the third approach: "limited access." This would provide sewers where the plan calls for medium and high density clusters, few sewers anywhere else. Cost: $30.50 per capita. In the low density areas septic tanks would have to be used and this would tend to retard development. Eventually, the planners acknowledge, the sewer system should embrace all the areas but until then the limited access system would not only be more economical, it would itself mold the development pattern.

The argument, of course, is not without a few holes. The sanitary engineer, in his comments on the report, was quick to point out that the reliance on septic tanks as a deterrent poses a number of problems, including health. He also bridled at the proposition that follow-ing regular policy would result in unnecessarily large sewer facilities. ("I have yet to see an over-designed sewer.") His chief objection was to the idea of manipu-lating the diameter of sewer pipes to control develop-ment. This would mean the complete stoppage of development until the overall development plan was worked up and adopted. He did concede, however, that *if* there were a good plan the engineers could design a more economical system.

STORM drainage is another cost item that cluster development can reduce. For one thing, there is less runoff with cluster. Conventional develop-ment, with its many miles of street surface, lays down an impervious surface on a great amount of land; this

Villiage Green: view of houses from edge of common area.

19

catches a greater amount of rainfall, over the total area, and makes necessary many more linear feet of storm sewers, curbs and gutters. At $15 or $16 per linear foot, these improvements add up to quite a charge.

Conventional development not only increases the run-off; it greatly cuts down the capacity of the natural drainage system to deal with the runoff. Flood plains and marshy areas, for example, are a wonderful sponge; but by diking and filling them there is quick commercial gain to be had. Later, when the inevitable floods come, the bill will be presented—not to the developer, but to the residents of the community—and much more concrete will have to be laid down to improve drainageways in areas that should not have been built upon in the first place.

Cluster development concentrates the building where the drainage problem can be most efficiently handled and leaves the bulk of the drainage system alone. Nature handles these things pretty well and if its own plan is respected there can be a saving in money and a gain in aesthetics. A free-flowing stream is an excellent storm sewer and it looks much better than a concrete channel.

One of the most notable examples of this kind of planning is that for the Reston development, and it is in Fairfax County that it is going up. The Reston plan calls for large-scale storm sewer facilities in the areas of high density, but it places great emphasis on keeping as much of the drainage network in its natural state as possible; rather than lining many of them with concrete, as in conventional practice, they want to have the drainageways stabilized by ferns and trees. To the county planners, this is exactly the approach they would like to see for the whole area.

Conveniently enough for illustration, Fairfax County is also outstanding for the opposite approach. Its public works department has been notable in its insistence on concrete drainageways and, not unexpectedly, the response to the planners' report was critical. In his opinion, wrote engineer B. C. Arasmussen, "the ultimate drainage improvements necessary within the stream valley flood plains would cost as much under the plan for suburban cluster, and in all probability exceed, the cost, as it would under the present type of development that you refer to as suburban sprawl."

As for Reston plan, he thought that many of the drainageways that the planners hoped to preserve in their natural state should be stabilized (i.e., with concrete). With large lot development, however, "there would be less land disturbed during the actual construction of residences, and this, in turn, would reduce the amount of runoff and silt loads that the streams would be expected to carry."

The conflict that Fairfax County illustrates so sharply is to be found in communities everywhere but there seems to be increasing support for the anti-concrete point of view, and from engineers as well as planners. Water resource studies made for the northeastern Illinois metropolitan area are a case in point: on the basis of the drainage problems of the area, the development pattern recommended calls for a higher concentration of development where topography and soil conditions are right, leaving the other areas in their natural state as much as possible.

This is cluster on the grand scale and it is the kind that planners especially like. The vision of order it promises is at the root of their growing concern over the drainage network. The economic and conservation arguments are convenient, but ancillary; what the planners see in the network is a way of structuring the whole growth pattern of the region.

On the smaller community scale the interdependence of cluster and the drainage network becomes more compelling. It is something we can see. Wooded stream valleys and such, of course, are desirable for any kind of development but they are particularly important for cluster. If prospective homeowners are to be sold on the idea of less private space in favor of more common space, that space has got to be attractive.

A stream turned into a concrete sluice doesn't enhance the looks of any subdivision; in a cluster development it is ludicrous. Our eye, as well as our mind, tells us that something is wrong.

BUT there are still a lot of engineers who love concrete. In California, most notably, they have a great propensity for lining every watercourse in concrete, and when highway engineers see a stream along the right of way, they are prone to rip-rap it into order with vast quantities of rock. In many cases, of course, the flood hazard demands such artificial improvements, but it does seem to have become such a habit that it is applied automatically, even when the natural channel can handle the load.

The dry creeks so characteristic of California are not much to look at at first glance, but as Santa Barbara County is finding out, with some judicious planting and clearing, they can make excellent walkways within developments and fine connectors between them. This function, furthermore, can make them effective in

Cluster economics are visible in this street scene in Manassas, Virginia. On one side are the town houses of Georgetown South; on the other a colony of twenty ranchers. One rancher takes up the linear space of three town houses. The ranchers rent for $90 to $95 a month. Monthly payment for the purchase of a two-bedroom town house: $88.

handling the occasional flash floods. Where flooding would be a problem, planners find that the careful planting of water-absorbent trees like sycamores and willows can achieve the necessary stabilization. In some cases this would not be enough to take care of the runoff on a new subdivision; to meet this problem planners would like the engineers to designate areas that would be susceptible to floods. Planners could then route new developments around such areas.

The need to revise engineering criteria is going to be further heightened as developers turn to the hills. The valley floors are pretty well used up and the flat land that is left is fetching fierce prices. Developers are now using hilly land that they would not have touched ten years ago, and they are learning a great many things about terracing and the handling of slopes. As they work up into the foothills they are finding that economics forces them to think of cluster.

The standards for conventional development of hilly tracts are prohibitive for all save very expensive houses. Planners feel these standards unnecessarily high, but they do see a benefit. The stiffer the standards are for conventional the more appetite developers have for cluster.

"We can extract a lot from these fellows now," says one county planner, "They have been coming in here all the time sounding me out about going up into the hills and they can't see any other way except cluster. Just take the sewers. They can't use septic tanks up there. They have to put in sewers and it is terribly expensive unless they can group the houses on the knolls and cut down the sewer runs. This is just what we would like them to do for all sorts of reasons. Roads, for example. We would like to see the hillsides left as natural as possible and so, for economics, would the developer."

But convincing the engineers is uphill too. Cluster or conventional, their standards for hillside roads remain quite high and, to assure access for fire trucks and evacuation, they insist on roads, curbs, and gutters of a size which many planners believe simply doesn't make sense. By clustering and the use of loop streets, planners point out, builders can vastly reduce the amount of earth moving — which is to say, the desecration of the topography — and still insure decent traffic circulation. In some areas the engineers have found that a reduction in width to, say, 20 foot roadways with 10 foot shoulders, would handle the peak loads they worry about; in more cases than not, however, they resist, and they still don't like cul-de-sacs. The new pressures for more hillside development will undoubtedly lead engineers to think of revising their standards. But it is going to be a slow process.

LET us be fair to the engineers. The resistance we have been talking about is the other side of a virtue. The engineer feels that he has a paramount responsibility to safeguard the public, and he has learned to be suspicious of any request for variance. For years builders have been trying to get standards changed, and not always for the most admirable reasons; the engineer can't be blamed if he looks on the cluster idea as a new gimmick for developers to do things they couldn't get away with otherwise.

The fact remains that the sheer process of getting engineers' and officials' approval for cluster projects constitutes a large economic factor in itself. An unconscionable amount of time has been consumed between the inception of many cluster projects and the final go-ahead from the local government. The new planned unit ordinances are a help, but what most say is that a developer can get approval of a new kind of project if the officials think he should get approval. The ordinances do not necessarily cut down the amount of parleying back and forth between builders, engineers, planners and officials. Sometimes they magnify it.

As communities get more experience with cluster development, many of the troublesome questions will be cleared up. But a more positive approach is needed: the processing should be expedited as a carrot for developers. Whatever the defects of conventional subdivisions for developers, it is the easy way as far as the civic machinery is concerned, and this has a great bearing on developers' costs. Each month that capital is tied up means higher costs—and a declining interest in projects that depart from the conventional.

Developers could do a lot to help if they would spend a little more money on their initial site planning. Platting a conventional FHA subdivision is such a cut and dried matter that many developers have been in the habit of having a civil engineer do all the work on the site plans, landscaping and all. Applied to cluster development, however, this penny-pinching can produce some pretty bad plans, and civic officials have been quite right to insist on changes and redrafts. Some of the most encouraging data encountered in this study, we should add, were the plans that *didn't* get built.

Less encouraging was the number of times that professional site planners were not brought in until it was obvious the initial cut rate plan wouldn't work very well. (Several of the best plans shown in this report began as rescue jobs.) A good site plan almost invariably produces savings far beyond whatever extra fee is involved; it would provide even more savings if such a plan had been drawn up in the first place. Good aesthetics, to repeat, make good economics.

From England comes this notable lesson in adaptation, St. Mary's Close. The developer, Durham Cathedral, had a four acre tract in the old and unusually attractive village of Shincliffe. Architect Donald Insall's task was to analyze the elements that made it so attractive and embody them in the *project. He succeeded. The layout, which places 29 houses around a common green, conveys a fine sense of place. But it is not at all quaint. The houses are clean and functional. No thatched roofs; no leaded glass panes; no olde street lamps. It was the essence of the village that he caught.*

Chapter III

THE COMMUNITY'S ATTITUDE

Ｏ N economic grounds alone, to recapitulate, cluster development makes sense not only for the developer and the homeowner, but for the community itself. It is one thing to document the case, however; it is quite another to sell it. When it comes to a specific project in a specific locality, the amount of resistance the cluster idea can generate sometimes reaches extraordinary proportions.

A sharp illustration of the basic obstacles is furnished by the efforts of real estate man Norman Blankman. About five years ago Blankman bought the 530 acre Whitney estate in Old Westbury, Long Island, and shortly after became excited about the possibilities of the cluster idea. He asked architect Victor Gruen to draw up such a plan for the Whitney estate.

Under the prevailing zoning of Old Westbury, 236 single homes could be put on the property. To do this, however, the plan would have called for covering virtually the entire tract; most of the trees would have to be chopped down and the golf course graded away for homes. The open spaces that the residents had long taken for granted would be no more.

The Gruen plan was to build 283 town houses in a series of clusters, concentrated on about seven acres of the total. Through this concentration the rest of the tract could be left open. In addition, the existing golf course would have been left and a second one would have been built, as well as leaving the lake and walkways.

The plan won high praise from architects and planners. Unfortunately, however, they lived somewhere else. In the town itself, initial reaction was mixed and cautious. The town officials retained a planning consultant to make a report on the feasibility of cluster for the town.

At a climactic public meeting, Blankman and Gruen presented their case. The consultant delivered his report; it was favorable. The late Hugh Pomeroy and the writer spoke about the advantages of the cluster principle and how the town could insure the permanence of the open space. But the opposition had been building and it became apparent that it was strongly emotional. If Blankman was so keen on this scheme, went the questions, what's the catch in it? Suppose he changed his mind about the open space? And those $60,000 houses — suppose people didn't buy them? And if they did, what kind of people would they be?

Tempers flared, and at about 11 P.M. the meeting was on the verge of breaking up into fisticuffs. Several weeks later the town officials voted against the zoning.

In September, 1963, Blankman sold 280 acres of the estate to the New York Institute of Technology for about $2,000,000. This may now be subtracted from the tax rolls.

Three points are worth noting. First, the developer was the first to broach the idea. There had been no previous urging of the cluster idea by the town's staff planners for there were none. Second, the matter had to be thrashed out in a meeting open to all comers. Experience in other communities indicates that such affairs are usually doomed to be free-for-alls; they can't result in positive approval, for no vote is involved, but the ill will they generally arouse can easily inhibit the town fathers from giving the approval. Developer Carl Freeman, who has had considerable success in selling garden apartment projects to Washington, D.C. suburbs, makes it a rule to meet with key committees of local groups rather than the full membership.

Third, it is not the old guard that gives the trouble so much as the newcomers — than whom no people are more apprehensive about the character of newcomers. To the newly arrived, large lot zoning is security against the people one leaves behind; change the rules and who knows what kind of low income riff-raff might not come in. In the case of Old Westbury one could reason that Blankman's prices — $60,000 and up per house — would keep them out, zoning or not, but

HUDSON RIVER

Blankman's cluster proposal for Tenafly.

reason does not help very much once the issue has become an emotional one.

BLANKMAN tried again. This time he bought a 276 acre tract in Tenafly, New Jersey. Its location was superb; only a few miles from the George Washington bridge, and it was bordered on one side by the Palisades Interstate Parkway. As the last big open space in the area available for development it had been zoned for one acre lots. Architect Ulrich Franzen drew up a striking plan which would use the bulk of the area for a golf course; town houses, 300 in all, would be grouped in five circular clusters, each with its own swimming pool. The houses, priced around $60,000, would be sold on the condominium plan, and the owners would jointly own and maintain the open space and the golf course. To explain all this and how it would benefit the town, Blankman had a special brochure prepared and sent to all of the 4,200 families in the town.

Wildly revolutionary, many townspeople thought, highly impractical. It so happens that Radburn lies only eight miles away and a visit could have answered many of the questions raised. It might as well have been on the other side of the moon. The idea congealed that cluster had never been tried, and wouldn't work if it were.

A town meeting was scheduled for October 2, 1962. The opposition, which had retained a public relations man to help organize things, prepared energetically, and at the meeting launched an attack that made the

Westbury meeting seem placid by comparison. Everyone had come primed with questions, and hour after hour Blankman and Franzen were bombarded with them. They did the best they could but the odds were hopeless. Blankman withdrew the proposal.

One by-product of this unhappy affair is a virtual syllabus of the objections laymen can raise about cluster. Some of the questions were highly particular to the situation — the earlier failure at Westbury was a special favorite — but they are the kind that developers and planners must be prepared to answer, or, ideally, anticipate so well they won't have to be asked at all. Here, from the written record, is a sampling.

What, if any, is the possibility of the golf course being sub-divided sometime in the future or possibly being sold and replaced by apartment or high rise buildings?

Is this democracy whereby you take town's usual public land and close it up?

How many of these homes do you have to sell before you will build the first "cluster"? What happens if you cannot sell all 300 homes?

Mr. Blankman — You say now the golf course and certain maintenance will be maintained by the organization. Since you are not a Tenafly resident, once you have made your profit and decide to sell, what guarantee that it will be kept to the liking of Tenafly residents that are here to stay?

Will the total tax return to the Borough of the "cluster plan" be equal to the return from individual homes?

What person would want to invest 55 or 60 thousand on a home with the exact or almost exact same plan as his 299 neighbors? People of intelligence in this age of conformity sometimes would like to try to retain some vestige of individuality. The idea of repetition, no matter how esthetically different or better, is still repetition. It smacks to me of Bensonhurst or Kew Gardens on a glorified scale.

Why have there been no architectural and scenic pictures to show what the cluster dwellings actually look like instead of just floor plans?

What precedent would be set for the rest of our town if cluster housing is approved for Mr. Blankman?

Has there been a successful cluster project up to now, including golf course and with homes at prices of $50 or $60,000, or is Tenafly the guinea pig?

Is it fair to assume that as a prudent businessman you were encouraged in your plan by someone in authority before you bought this property?

Open ditches to control drainage! Is that safe? Brownstones in New York City — Are not most slums now? Didn't most people move to the country to get away from this?

Your brochure states that Regional Plan Association, Mr. Tankel, and Senator Harrison Williams, have approved this project. Have they approved it for Tenafly?

What assurance is there that these individual residential units are a saleable commodity, and that they can compete with rental apartments and individual dwellings in the housing market?

Is the membership of the club limited?

Would the demands on Borough services be greater in the cluster plan or by conventional subdivision. What would the difference be?

The Township of Old Westbury rejected a similar plan. It is inconceivable that such a rejection could have been accepted without a questioning of the reasons.

Will this be submitted to a public referendum?

Are we not putting the cart before the horse? Ask the audience whether they are in favor of changing the present zoning which this project requires.

What provisions could be made to insure *the prevention of ANY buildings on the rest of the land?*

Are there any local residents in on this deal?

What benefits do existing residents get from a private park and private golf course?

Mr. Chairman: Are you concerned about the interests of the residents of Tenafly? If so, ask if the people in this auditorium want Cluster Homes in this town or not. WE ALL HEARD THE FACTS.

While the Tenafly fracas was raging there was an unusual turnabout in nearby Hillsborough, New Jersey. The cluster zoning ordinance which had been passed the year before was revoked — not because the cluster principle didn't work but because it threatened to work too well.

The cause of it all was Village Green, the development described earlier in Chapter Two. The subdivision was a good one. Even before it was finished, however, there were second thoughts on the part of some of the townspeople. Hillsborough would be the only town in the area offering this advanced method of subdivision. Would this not make it too attractive to developers? A cluster subdivision might be better for the town than a conventional subdivision, but what many Hillsborough people wanted most was no more subdivisions of any kind. The whole subject became a violent political issue and an anti-cluster member of the council became mayor. In February, 1962, the cluster provision of the ordinance was revoked.

RESISTANCE is more than a suburban phenomenon. The city of Milwaukee furnishes a vivid example of how far people can go against their own interests to resist something new. Along Milwaukee's gold coast, by the side of Lake Michigan, was a small tract of about seven acres. It was zoned for single family houses and had indeed already been platted for such a subdivision.

Planner William Nelson came up with a design that would be much more in keeping with the upper income character of the neighborhood—an interesting combination of 16 town houses around a courtyard and two apartment buildings set on a lakeside slope.

The developers went to considerable pains to sell all the neighborhood on the idea. One move which they felt quite successful was to stage a tour of the property for the residents. They set up an exhibit in a tent on the site and at strategic locations on the site had large sketches showing what the view would be from that point. They also put yellow tapes on all the trees which were being saved. Lemonade was served and there were people on hand to answer questions. The exhibit was open for four days.

Most of those who came appeared convinced, but not enough came. The planning commission seemed to be unanimously in favor but after the public hearing it was apparent that there was a dedicated "anti" group and because of their opposition the project is stillborn.

The charge, as elsewhere, is that the cluster project would hurt surrounding property values. Evidence is mounting that the effect is more likely to be the opposite, but for some time to come many a community is going to take a lot of convincing.

SO far we have been talking of projects which have run into unusual opposition. Let us look now on several instances where the community problem has been resolved more easily. An outstanding

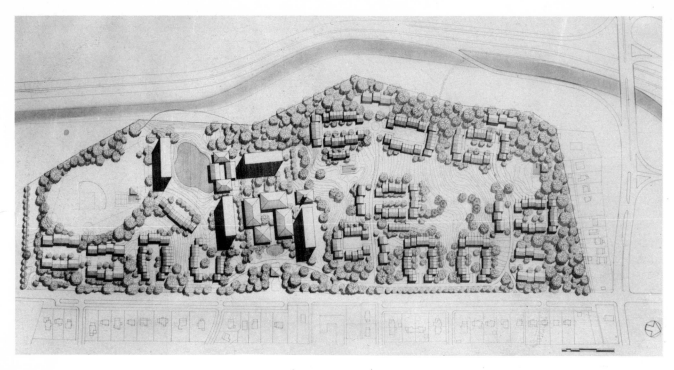

Site plan for Cross Keys village. Tower apartments and village shops are in center.

example is the procedure by which James Rouse got approval for his Cross Keys project for the Roland Park section of Baltimore. The site had been part of the Baltimore Country Club's golf course; the club offered it for sale when the city acquired half the course for a school. Rouse proposed a cluster project. The club would have architectural control over the design of the houses and the overall layout.

Roland Park, which had been launched just before the turn of the century as a model community, should have been a very hard nut to crack. It is a conservative upper income neighborhood, and ordinarily such a project would have sent the residents to the barricades. In addition to an unusual design it was to be a rental project and if there is one thing that incites the animosity of established communities it is the threat of apartment units, the defects of apartment dwellers, the unconscionable load they put on the community, their lack of allegiance, etc. etc.

In this case, however, Rouse started with a number of favorable factors; he was, for one thing, a well-known community leader and a salesman of compelling, if low key, impact. Before filing a zoning application or making any presentation to city officials, Rouse organized a series of neighborhood meetings in the Roland Park area.

At each meeting he would discuss the alternatives. As is customary in virtually every cluster presentation, he showed the kind of project that would be called for by the existing zoning. It was stark and ugly.

He presented the alternative. There would be no increase in the number of units, yet much more open space. The trees and slopes wouldn't be cut away; the traffic pattern wouldn't overload the nearby streets; the project's service facilities would make it reasonably self-sufficient and not a burden on the community.

Rouse did not force his audiences into a premature stance with a take-it-or-leave-it plan. He wanted to work it out in cooperation with them, he said, and would like their comments and suggestions. The response was friendly and several of the ideas useful enough to put Rouse into the happy position of being able to incorporate them into the plan. The clincher was his agreement to enforceable deed restrictions that would guarantee the integrity of the plan. By the time the planning commission meeting came around, the residents were thoroughly sold. With no commotion whatsoever the necessary variances were approved.

Rouse is such a persuasive fellow that he might have gotten the plan through whether he used this procedure or not. But there may be a lesson here of fairly wide applicability. A new idea is especially hard to take when it has to be taken all at once. There is a minimum time element necessary for digesting a new idea and this cannot usually be short-circuited by a blitz of expert testimony. The writer has seen a number of meetings where you could almost sense the exact moment in which the citizenry's back went up; if it is all too much too fast a resistance hardens that is impervious to logical argument, and it is with relish that townspeople will say that *their* town is different and they don't give a damn what the experts can prove by plans somewhere else. The let's-work-it-out-together approach runs the risk of being disingenuous but it can offer an excellent climate for the indispensable job of exposition.

In the areas where cluster development has developed with the least resistance, there seem to be two principal ·denominators:

1. The local government has been fairly sophisticated in planning matters and has had a considerable history behind it of land use studies, or successful fights for other innovations.

2. The cluster idea was advanced initially by the community's planning agency rather than by developers.

Monterey County, California, is a good case in point. This scenic county, among other things is notable for being the first in the country to zone its roads against billboards, and, has had a very vigorous planning movement widely supported by various civic organizations. Several years ago an open space study, commissioned by the county, strongly urged the cluster idea. The planners pointed out that if there was to be any hope of open space conservation there would have to be an alternative to the typical land wasting pattern of development. The report went on to sketch, with hypothetical examples, how cluster could be that alternative. Such a pattern, the report pointed out, would make it far easier for conservationists to achieve the larger open space network they were pushing for.

This was a very important educational step, for what it did was to harness the interest of the very kinds of people to whom the idea of development was almost an anathema. They pushed for cluster development, to stretch a point, because they didn't like development at all.

The report also had considerable effect on developers themselves. One landowner was particularly intrigued. He had had considerable trouble before with local zoning boards and he had a very large tract that he planned to develop. This tract, a beautiful mass of hills and savanna, was the view out of many picture windows in the area and he could be sure that the conventional

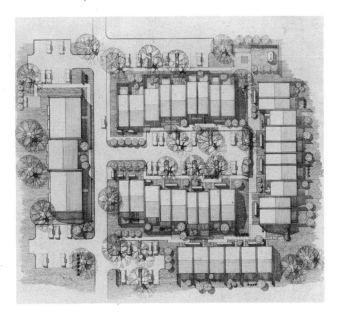

Detail of Cross Keys court.

development he was planning would rouse a tempest of opposition.

Intrigued by the hypothetical examples, he went to the same planners that had done the report, Hall and Goodhue of Monterey, and asked them to draw up a cluster plan for the tract. The plan they drew up, High Meadow, was a superb job and when it was announced in the newspapers it was greeted with considerable enthusiasm. It also won an award from the American Institute of Architects as the finest subdivision plan of the year.

Not unlike the Gruen plan for Old Westbury, the High Meadow plan has been one of those that has had a considerable impact without ever getting built. For a number of reasons, including some unresolved decisions about the location of the new highway, the landowner has not yet gone ahead. In the meantime, however, county planners have been working with developers with increasing success, and two later projects designed by Hall and Goodhue are now going up.

We are, to repeat, in a fast moving situation. For some time to come the problem of community resistance will be a tough one in many areas and a strong educational effort will be called for. But the ice has been broken. The most persuasive argument is a new cluster development that citizens and officials can look at, and now that more and more are going up, in most urban areas of the U.S. the evidence is close at hand.

Chapter IV

THE MARKET PLACE

THE crucial vote is in the market place and the returns are now coming in. In Appendix A we have tabulated the available sales data for most of the cluster developments that have been going up. Comparing sales figures, let it be noted, is a bit like comparing apples and oranges. Some developments have sold extremely well, some poorly; in either case it is difficult to sort out cause and effect and to say to what degree the cluster factor was responsible.

Nevertheless, there is a constancy of sorts. Where there have been no unusual adverse factors, cluster developments have sold as well as conventional developments in the same price range in the area and in a number of cases have sold much better. The number of cluster developments up so far is not large enough to give definite proof but they are spread across so wide a price range, are found in so many areas and of so many architectural styles that we already have a pretty fair test of the basic question of whether or not people will buy cluster housing. On this point, the verdict seems rather clear. They will.

The acceptance curve, furthermore, seems to be accelerating. One of the biggest drawbacks has been psychological — the well-known "fact" that Americans are too keen on the individual homestead to reverse themselves. Such an assumption can be proof against reality for quite a long time. But there comes a point when it can no longer stand up.

The critical point is not a successful market test. That has already taken place. Given a free choice, a considerable number of people have already chosen to buy cluster housing in preference to conventional housing. The critical point is when this fact becomes generally apparent to the citizenry.

That time is not quite yet. You will still hear people maintain that cluster probably won't work, even though there are cluster developments in their area which very demonstrably are working. But the situation is changing rapidly and just how rapidly is illustrated by the remarkable impact of just one development.

One of the nation's largest builders, Kaufman and Broad, is in the final stages of a town house project on the flat fields of Orange County, just southeast of Los Angeles — the very heartland of the ranch house. The project, Huntington Continental, has row houses and of the neo-Georgetown type rather than California style. They are packed close together. They are inexpensive, starting at $10,000, yet looking at the project, you could deduce from known factors that they clearly would not sell, particularly so when you look at the flags flying from the competing ranch house developments going up all over the place. But there are all those people coming to look at the model houses — and they are buying.

The success of this Kaufman and Broad project has had a tremendous impact. Some architects and planners express horror ("Will set back housing 20 years" . . .) but consumers feel it is a lot of house for the money, and they are the consumers who make up the fat slice of the market. Builders in the area see a bandwagon: they've been scrapping their conventional plans and rushing through town house projects. They have been doing it at such a rate that the FHA had to send a special task force to cope with the applications.

WHAT kind of people make up the market? The market data we have been able to assemble indicates that people who buy cluster housing don't seem to be much different from anybody else. As far as income is concerned, one could reason that cluster, like so many new concepts, would do best in the beginning with people of high educational and income levels and that there would have to be a trickle-down effect before it was ready for the mass market. This does not seem to be the case. Several of the most successful developments have been in the $40,000-and-up range and have made something of a point of being for taste makers. As the Kaufman and Broad project demonstrates, however, several of the most spectacular sales have been at the other end of the price scale. One of these, Colonial Park in Louisville, Kentucky, attracted

Huntington Continental model houses.

Sales exhibits stress cluster advantages.

so many would-be buyers that the news brought developers from all over the country to Louisville to see what was up. As it turned out, most of the applicants could not qualify for the FHA financing but the potential demand uncovered was not lost on developers.

Here and there some interesting differences have been noticed. In the San Jose area, Eichler Homes, Inc., was selling a cluster development at the same time it was selling a conventional subdivision in the same price range. The cluster project sold slower, but what was most interesting was the difference in the purchasers. Those who bought cluster houses tended to have a somewhat higher income, be older, and have more children. Most significant, they tended to be people who had lived in the San Jose area, many in conventional tract homes. The purchasers in the conventional subdivision tended to be newcomers.

Edward Eichler thinks this difference is tied up with the need for security. "People in transit — people who haven't sunk roots in an area — want the security of the known. The people who have already had roots in the area and feel more established are psychologically more prepared to go for cluster. I think the problem is that we have trained people for too long that they should aspire to detached homes. In the city the town house is no longer a problem, but it still is in suburbia."

In other areas, however, barriers seem to be crumbling quite rapidly. In the Washington area, for example, the Georgetown South development is proving to have a strong appeal with newcomers in precisely the middle income and occupational groups generally regarded as having a strong impulse for conventional suburban homes. Whatever psychic drives they may have for a lot of their own, they seem able to sublimate them quite successfully.

To merchandise the cluster idea developers in different parts of the country have arrived at much the same appeals; in many cases the similarity of the promotional material, not to mention the developments themselves, is so marked that one composite brochure could do for the lot of them.

By far and away the most important single element in sales success, of course, is the house itself and its price, or rather, the monthly payment. The marginal advantages that cluster offers, however, can become extremely important in a tight competitive situation and it is on these advantages that developers' promotion is concentrated. Here, in brief, are the major themes.

Cluster is the coming thing. Developers habitually advertise any subdivision as a new way of life; in the case of cluster, however, they have some real explaining to do, and on the whole they have managed to do it quite effectively. Salesmen report that with few exceptions prospects grasp the idea quickly and their questions reveal little skepticism. Here is some characteristic exposition:

"Hailed by forward-looking municipal authorities, the cluster-type plan . . . provides for grouping the homes on individual king-size plots averaging 15,000 sq. ft. in three horseshoe clusters, thus preserving the remaining 44 acres as a park and recreational area." (Village Green, New Jersey)

"The Cluster has been hailed by municipal planners across the nation as an exciting new concept for lovelier, more gracious community design. Yet the cluster is actually a modern adaptation of the age-old pattern of the villages that dot the European countryside. Five homes are grouped together around areas of green

parkland, and the total community is set like a jewel in a protective ring of open countryside. The open space . . . literally recreates the charm of a European village." (Georgetown East, Cedarburg, Wisconsin)

In trying to establish that cluster is the coming thing, so far most developers have not bothered to knock the conventional subdivision, possibly because many of them are still building conventional subdivisions. In the

Huntington Continental site plan: elemental cluster.

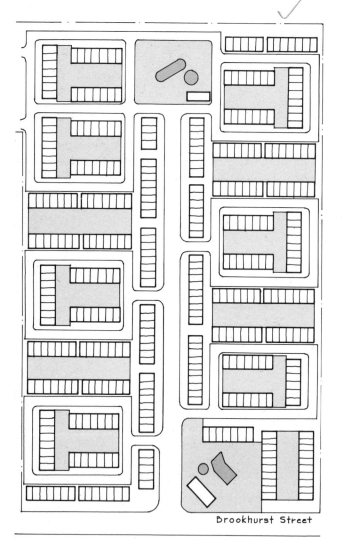

Brookhurst Street

future, however, they are likely to indulge in more fighting copy on this score; there have already been a few strong intimations that conventional developments are for squares. Cluster developments are for smart young moderns, influentials, and pacesetters. *"Cluster in IN! . . . the answer to rows upon rows of homes assembled, in the appropriately named 'gridiron' pattern. The cluster abolishes the monotony and regimentation of the normal subdivision."* (Georgetown East) . . .

"Gone are the unimaginative grid rows of homes . . . cramped concrete-fenced backyards . . . stereotyped front lawns . . ." (College Green, Fullerton, Cal.)

Cluster produces more house for the money. This appeal is used for almost all cluster developments but is expressed most forcibly for the town house variety.

"How in this era of rising prices can Huntington Continental give you so much luxury for so little cost? . . . take for example the ingredient of land. The ever-rising and almost prohibitive price of property is one of the highest cost factors involved in the construction of ordinary-planned homes. By contrast, Townhouse Living utilizes land to the fullest extent, giving you an unusual combination of complete home ownership, substantial savings and recreational advantages formerly impossible to attain except through estate-size ownership."

Instead of muting the fact of the party wall, developers are now making a big point of it. The most frequently cited advantage is the savings in initial cost; another is the increased shelter. Thus Georgetown South: "And best of all, heating costs are literally cut in half by the extra warmth and wind protection you get in a townhouse, with the official gas company estimate at about $8.00 per month average."

Cluster Offers a Great Recreational Environment for Children and Adults — The literature aimed at younger marrieds bears down heavily on the wholesomeness and safety the open space network provides. *"Your son doesn't put his life in the hands of a motorist whenever he backs into a traffic-free cul-de-sac to catch a fly ball. Anyway, it is unlikely that he could hit the ball out of the park."* "Your children grow up healthy and strong, surrounded by worthwhile friends and experiencing all the wholesome advantages of superior living."

On this point, developers try to leave little to the imagination of the home buyer. The first thing that most of them build, along with the model houses, is the recreation center and swimming club, and where the subdivision is to feature a golf course, the course gets built first. It is a rather odd sight, in fact, to see some of these subdivisions in their initial stages. Some look remarkably like movie sets; even though there might be only a few houses completed, at stage front there may be an olympic-size swimming pool, snack bar and cabana club going full tilt for a handful of families.

It may be costly, but it does dress up the house. In one new subdivision, where only a few houses have been occupied so far, the writer was intrigued to note a troupe of happy children continually cycling back and forth through the underpass and playing on a beautifully manicured greensward. They couldn't have been a better advertisement if they had been hired.

Cluster Offers a Rich Community Life. Developers capitalize heavily on the group-living aspects offered by the common green, the propinquity of helpful neighbors, and the democratic self-government of the homeowners association.

Cluster Offers Privacy. At the same time, developers emphasize privacy even more heavily. In this best of all possible worlds, the homeowners have companionship when they want it; a retreat insulated from the bustle about when they want that. *"Togetherness with complete privacy,"* one brochure puts it.

The design does it. *"It is the right of every individual to get away from it all, 'go upstairs to bed',"* . . . *"and only in a double-level home can the frustrations and gold fish exposures of the stereotype 'ranch house' be avoided and the blessings of solitude be enjoyed."* (Heather Hills, Louisville, Ky.)

The arguments are not entirely specious; in the cluster layouts of the town house type there is usually a clear separation between public and private space. The patio is not only private, it is generally fenced from view and, although the size is much smaller, there is far more real privacy than in a large lot that is not enclosed. When two adjacent families each have friends in for a barbecue, there is less apt to be the merging problem that the open backyard of conventional developments invites. (Shall we ask them to join the party just for drinks? Will they expect supper?) Good fences, as they say, make good neighbors.

For other reasons as well, the patio is being featured more and more heavily. In addition to its function as an outdoor play and living area, the patio has the great advantage of extending the apparent size of the interior. In the most frequent type of layout, the kitchen is at the front of the first floor and often is separated from the living room only by an island, thus giving a considerable visual sweep from the front of the house on back through the sliding glass doors to the patio. In the perspective of the brochure illustrations, the expanse is so great you can hardly see the end of the patio for the distance.

Cluster means Freedom from Care. In a reverse way, the tyranny of the suburban lawn is becoming a big talking point for cluster, and the higher the density and the smaller their lots the more developers push the advantages. *"The good life,"* one interprets it, *"with time to enjoy it."*

Many cluster communities not only relieve the homeowners of any mowing burden, but take care of the outside of his house, including roof repairs and painting, and some throw in such services as daytime supervision of childrens' area. Translated in terms of freedom and leisure, it makes quite a point. To quote Eichler Homes:

"The management of Pomeroy West cares for it all. The landscaping, the community center and pool, even your home. Whether it's weeding or watering, repainting or repairs, you have no maintenance worries. Everything is done for you. This gives you time for a weekend at the lake, or a month in the Orient, or just more relaxing moments in your own private gardens. There are no cares of homeownership here, only the rewards."

This appeal would seem to be most appropriate for developments in the upper price brackets; these usually have a stronger representation of older couples whose children have grown up and who had become somewhat disenchanted with the operation of their suburban establishment. There are signs, however, that there are

Hard sell for a conservative market: newspaper insert prepared by Milwaukee developer Clarence Dittmar.

quite a few younger couples who are not keen to take on such an establishment to begin with.

Cluster means trees. Talks with homeowners reveal that trees are a much bigger market factor than is generally recognized. Many developers still think it's cheaper to cut down everything in the way and then plant saplings. But people have trouble imagining what these will look like 30 years hence: they like trees they can see now—big, old trees—and just a few can give a grace and sense of stability to a new tract that nothing else can match.

So far, however, developers have not made much of the point that cluster allows them to build around trees instead of chopping them down. The trees themselves make the point best, but several developers have tried such merchandising devices as attaching special placards for emphasis. Other than this very little imagination has been shown.

ALL in all, the total impact of these different appeals seems to be growing. In part, of course, the success of cluster is due to a fairly strong overall market for all housing; and there is no assurance that it will continue strong; indeed, there are a number of indications that there could be real trouble ahead. If this were to come about, cluster development would certainly be hurt; its relative performance, however, might well improve. Competition would be stiffer and the economic advantages of cluster over conventional could become all the more important.

The beginnings of the spiraling effect are already apparent. The recreational aspects of cluster, for example, are becoming a very important market factor. It is true, of course, that a recreational complex doesn't necessarily demand a cluster layout, but the two are so well adapted to each other that most cluster developments feature recreational facilities, and in home buyers' minds, too, they soon may become synonymous.

The day is very close at hand when a developer simply won't be able to compete unless he offers a full scale of recreational facilities. In some California communities that point has already been reached. Like electric kitchens and tile bathrooms, a swim club has become virtually indispensable. Some developers still hold out and grumble that they prefer to concentrate on giving the most house for the money. The argument rings a bit hollow, however, when the floor traffic in the model house is off because everybody seems to be flocking over to the competition's houses. When the market says that something is on its way to becoming part of the American way of life, the developers will be getting aboard.

Chapter V

THE LEGAL BASE

PLANNERS have never had any great doubts on the basic validity of cluster zoning. The courts have repeatedly upheld the right of a community to control density by specifying minimum lot sizes, and it would certainly seem reasonable that the community should be able to adjust these minimums if it gets compensating benefits from developers. Nevertheless, the issue has been clouded because of the trouble other kinds of ordinances have been having in the courts, most particularly, those requiring forced dedication of park land to the community or payment of money in lieu of land.

The issue that they raise is how far a community can go in exacting land from developers as a matter of course and in a number of cases courts have been ruling that communities have tried to exact too much. This is quite different from the cluster principle, with its voluntary exchange, but it is easy for laymen to confuse the two. What has been needed is a clear-cut test of a cluster ordinance. That test has now been made.

The setting for it could not be more appropriate. If you follow the track of the bulldozers moving north from Philadelphia and those moving south from New York, you will find that the last field of combat will be in the township of South Brunswick, New Jersey. Ten years ago, it was virtually all open. Then, almost overnight it seemed, a large development, Kendall Park, sprung up, putting 6,000 people where previously there had been scattered homes and farms. In the classic cycle of new suburbia, township officials found themselves with heavy demands for school and park sites. When they looked at the thirty-two square miles of open land that still remained, they grew understandably apprehensive. They called in consultant Robert Catlin to draw up a master plan. In his report Catlin strongly urged them to change their zoning rules before the next wave hit, and he recommended that they adopt a density zoning ordinance.

They had reason to be quick about it. Developer Kenneth Berg had acquired a 450 acre tract and had gotten approval of a conventional plan with 13,500 square foot minimum lots. Now he was ready to go ahead.

The township officials began conferring with Berg and his group to see if the plan could be reworked into something more along the cluster idea. Berg was amenable. To enable such plans for this and other subdivisions, the planning board recommended a density zoning ordinance. It was adopted on October 2, 1962. Here are key excerpts:

At the discretion of the Planning Board, a subdivider may be allowed to reduce the minimum lot size and dimension requirements in accordance with the provisions of this Ordinance, provided the following conditions are met:

(a) The resulting net lot density of the area to be subdivided shall be no greater than the net lot density of the said area without regard to the provisions of this Ordinance.

(b) All lands within the subdivision other than streets, building lots and private recreational areas shall be deeded to the Township for public purposes simultaneously with the granting of final subdivision approval.

Berg revised his plan. It still called for a basically conventional subdivision and the same number of detached houses but now the minimum lot sizes were reduced from 13,500 to 10,800 sq. ft. In exchange for this compression Berg would deed the open space for school and park sites.

During all of this time, needless to say, opponents were mustering. In September, they had managed to get 500 signatures on a petition against the density zoning ordinance. When the ordinance went through anyway, they turned to the courts. They brought suit against the township, charging that the ordinance was a set-up deal put through for the special interest of Berg. State statutes, they further charged, required uniformity within a zoning district and Brunswick Acres was a special case; the town's master plan report, furthermore, did not call for such zoning. *Chrinko vs. South Brunswick Township Planning Board* commenced.

On January 3, 1963, after extensive testimony by expert witnesses and others, Judge David D. Furman of the Superior Court handed down the decision. It was in favor of the cluster ordinance — strongly so. The opinion is so affirmative on each of the issues that it will be widely cited and may have considerable influence well beyond New Jersey.

The opinion is a broad one. It takes up the question of urban sprawl and whether there is a valid public purpose in conserving open space. In this respect, this opinion is a good example of the mutually supporting effect that various kinds of open space legislation can have; it cites, among other things, the passage of the New Jersey Green Acres act, and the findings of various studies.

Clearly, the court finds, there is a public purpose involved and local governments can properly adapt their ordinances to this end.

"Although the state zoning law does not in so many words empower municipalities to provide an option to developers for cluster or density zoning, such an ordinance reasonably advances the legislative purposes of securing open spaces, preventing overcrowding and undue concentration of population, and promoting the general welfare. Nor is it an objection that uniformity of regulation is required within a zoning district. Such a legislative technique accomplishes uniformity because the option is open to all developers within a zoning district, and escapes the vice that it is compulsory."

"Zoning ordinances in rapidly growing municipalities may be founded on an outmoded concept that houses will be built one at a time for individual owners in accordance with zoning regulations, with latitude for variances in hardship or other exceptional cases, and that the municipality can take steps whenever warranted to acquire school, park and other public sites. Such a gradual and controlled devolment is not practicable in many municipalities today. Confronted with a subdivision plan for several hundred homes in a tract meeting all water drainage, sanitation and other conditions, a municipality must anticipate school needs but without lands set aside for that purpose; it must anticipate a large population concentration without recreation areas, parks or green spaces, or lands for firehouses or other public purposes. Cluster or density zoning is an attempted solution, dependent, as set up in the South Brunswick zoning ordinance, upon the agreement of the large-scale developer whose specific monetary benefit may be only that he saves on street installation costs."

On the charge that the ordinance was for the benefit of the developer, the court held that the advantages to him seemed small, and in any case the ordinance wouldn't be bad for the town simply because it was good for the developer. "By overwhelming authority," the court observed, "otherwise valid legislation is not nullified because it accomplishes an incidental benefit to one or a few private individuals."

The opponents had charged that the ordinance deviated from the density zoning formula proposed for the master plan. "The legislative decision is the township's, not the planning consultant's," the court noted, adding that the testimony amply supported the modifications the township officials had made for the master plan report.

So far, so good. In taking up the public benefits, however, the court noted that the open land was to be dedicated to the township. The court itself did not hold that such dedication should be mandatory; the township had done this. The distinction, however, is blurry and there may possibly be a further ruling on this point in the higher courts.

It would be well if there were. New Jersey is on its way to establishing a fixed principle that cluster open spaces should be given to the municipality. More than elsewhere, cluster has been pushed as a way for communities to acquire open land without having to pay anything for it. Much of the land, of course, is used for playgrounds and parks for the subdivisions from which it was extracted. A good bit, however, makes a net addition to the community's overall land bank and can be drawn upon for future needs that may arise. One township estimates that it has already amassed land from developers that would have cost $125,000 at the market price. So successful has this kind of persuasion been that some communities see no need to tap New Jersey's Green Acres fund for matching open space grants. They'd have to put up some money.

All this certainly beats taxes. It has helped to sell the cause of cluster and the developers, figuring that if you can't beat 'em join 'em, have so far not been too disposed to quibble. And why, it could be asked, should anyone? A lot of open space has been saved and everyone's the better for it.

So be it. But what are good tactics at a given time don't necessarily make good law. Cluster development may indeed provide free park land for towns. To require that it always do so, however, is to ask too much, and not only on theoretical grounds, but practical ones as well. We can be sure that the home builders would eventually launch a strong counter attack on such requirements and on constitutional grounds they would very likely win.

Who *should* own the open space? To clarify this critical point let us go back a moment to the basic justification of cluster. The idea is to benefit people — primarily, the people who live in the developments. Other people in the community may benefit too, but this is a corollary, not the purpose.

What unifies these self interests is that a more effective use of the land can produce a better place to live in. An exchange is made: land ordinarily wasted on extensive streets, back yards and such is massed so that it is really usable for recreation and amenity. This common land is not a subtraction, to be given to somebody else; it is for the benefit of the home-buyers.

They're paying for it, after all. To say that the town is squeezing a gift out of the developer may sound like canny trading but it's not really his gift. The cost of the land has already been built into the price of the homes. The people who buy them are the ones who are paying for the open space.

Who benefits? If the residents do such dedication can be entirely fair. Long before cluster, communities have been requiring that a portion of each subdivision be deeded for school or park sites and the courts have sustained them. The justification, however, has been that such land is needed because of the new residents. Where the courts and common sense balk, is when the land is exacted to fulfill some other municipal purpose — such as a new fire house, or a town hall. All the taxpayers benefit; all of them should share in the cost. To charge the site against one subdivision is to charge a community-wide cost to one small segment.

To recapitulate: The community does derive benefits from the open spaces of cluster development; in considering the *physical* use of these spaces, however, it is the residents who have the primary equity.

I F we grant this proposition the question resolves itself into one of figuring which form of ownership and maintenance would work best. In the abstract, it is impossible to say, and that is why ordinances should not try to. There are several courses and which is best depends on the particulars of the circumstances.

The principal methods are:

1. municipal ownership
2. homeowners associations
3. special service districts
4. landlord maintenance

In many cases the interests of the home owners and those of the municipality may be best served by municipal ownership. Greenhaven '70 in Sacramento is an example. Here is a very large tract in a vacant section of the city which is being developed as a complete community in line with an overall plan sponsored by the city. For all practical purposes, the general public that will use the open spaces and the residents of the area will be one and the same. Free access to the commons raises no conflict of interest and the city park department is a logical mechanism for the maintenance of the area.

In other cases, particularly in smaller subdivisions, there can be a real conflict. The open spaces have been merchandised as part of the subdivision and to demand full public access raises a host of troublesome questions. If the public did use the interior open spaces to any considerable extent, the residents would feel cheated; conversely, if the public made little use, some members of the public could complain because their taxes were used to maintain the spaces.

In cases like this, the logical answer is to have the residents as a group own and maintain the land. As Chapter Six explains in more detail, there are tested mechanisms for this. The most common is a non-profit corporation composed of the homeowners. Another procedure is to set up a special governmental service district, the boundaries of which coincide with the subdivision. The district maintains the open space and has the power to levy assessments on the residents. This procedure has been used successfully in Connecticut, Colorado, and California.

But there need be no either-or proposition between public and private ownership. Both kinds of ownership can be combined, and for the same development. The great promise of cluster, indeed, can only be fulfilled if the various open spaces are conceived of as part of a whole rather than merely an accumulation of isolated areas. The open spaces of one subdivision are far more effective if they connect with public open spaces such as schools and parks and with the open spaces of other subdivisions. This approach calls for the use of several tools; the interior common of a subdivision, for example, might best be handled by a homeowners association. At the same time, the open space with a connective quality, such as a small stream valley, would probably be an element of the community's open space network and, in this case, dedication to the municipality would be in order. The walkways and bridle paths of such a network serve the self-interest of the residents of the subdivision because they are municipal in character.

THE municipality's soundest course, then, is to require guarantees that the space remain open, but to leave the door open as to the precise form of ownership to be used. This is the procedure embodied in what is probably the best state enabling act for cluster zoning. In 1963 the New York legislature clarified the town law by an act that is significant not only for its clarity but for the fact that it was hammered out to the satisfaction of municipal planners and of developers.

After a number of court cases had raised questions over the somewhat ambiguous provisions of earlier town law, the planners worked out a package which joined what the developers wanted — cluster legislation — with what they didn't — clearer authority for payment of money in lieu of land. The developers objected violently and in 1962 the bill died in committee. But the two parties could agree on cluster: after some protracted sessions in 1963 a version acceptable to both sides was easily passed. (See Appendix B.)

On the key question of open space ownership, here is the way the act reads: "In the event that the application of this procedure results in a plat showing land available for park, recreation, open space, or other municipal purposes directly related to the plat, then the planning board as a condition of plat approval may establish such conditions on the ownership, use, and maintenance of such lands as it deems necessary to assure the preservation of such lands for their intended purposes. The town board may require that such conditions shall be approved by the town board before the plat may be approved for filing."

WHEN it comes to the detailed wording of municipal ordinances, we find a variety of models and at this stage it is impossible to say which will prove the most workable. Appendix C contains the full text of a number of ordinances; they demonstrate the main approaches — and how many different ways there are to work to the same goal.

The most rudimentary ones, usually called density or cluster zoning, state that developers cannot put up any more homes than the zoning calls for in their district but that they can reduce lot sizes if the land saved is put into open space. Some ordinances frequently set formulae for the reductions; if present zoning calls for 15,000 square foot minimums, for example, lots can be reduced to 12,000 feet; from 10,000 to 8,000, and so on.

These are adequate for small cluster subdivisions but they are not geared to large ones of the "new town" type. It is these that planners would most like to encourage, and there is now a marked trend to ordinances that will encourage such developments. The nomenclature varies — community unit plan, planned residential development, planned unit development district — but basically they amount to an invitation.

The simplest of such ordinances ask the developer to come in and talk things over with the planners. The ordinances say in more or less words that the town wants to keep to the basic densities set by present zoning, but that if a developer assembles a big tract and wants to do a real job of community planning for it, the planners would be glad to consider adjusting the rules.

Such ordinances have the virtue of simplicity but they do beg the question of what changes will be permitted. When the ordinances do not specify any new rules of the game, developers can find themselves in very protracted negotiations, and seemingly minor stumbling blocks can lead to interminable haggling. Storm drainage strips, are an example. Where the terrain calls for them the developer has to provide them in any event. Question: should such strips, then, be considered part of the open space he gives in exchange for clustering, or over and above it? There are several different ways to resolve this question. The point is that a way should be agreed upon, as a matter of principle rather than case by case negotiation.

There seems to be a trend toward coupling the invitations to think big with some fairly specific guidelines. For the storm drainage question, for example, the code might specify that if the strips are incorporated into a landscape plan they could account for 50% of the open space required. Like any regulations which get into detail, these have the potential defect that they might freeze standards even though later experience might suggest changes. On balance, however, the existence of commonly recognized guidelines is a big advantage, and on the important variable of time can have a beneficial effect. In this respect, readers might particularly note the ordinances enacted by Baltimore County; their specifications constitute a well thought out manual and the emphasis is not on what developers can't do, but on the positive things they can do. And this, in sum, should be the thrust of all the ordinances.

Chapter VI

HOMEOWNERS ASSOCIATIONS

WHAT seems to trouble the layman most about cluster is the question of what's to be done with the open space. Who should own it? Take care of it? Pay the taxes?

In actual fact, these questions are the easiest to answer. This is not to say that they require little attention; in no aspect of cluster development is clear detailed, unambiguous procedure more important. But there has now been accumulated a considerable body of experience in the handling of common areas, and the basic principles are quite clear.

There have been a number of developments in the past that have featured common recreation or garden areas and which have set up homeowners associations to maintain them. Many date back to the twenties and thirties — Radburn, New Jersey, for example, the Country Club developments of J. C. Nichols in Kansas City. Some go back much further. Boston's Louisburg Square has been maintained by a homeowners association for over 125 years. New York's Gramercy Park was set up by real estate operator Samuel Ruggles in 1831. Property arrangements differ but in one important respect most of these associations are alike: they are still going strong.

To find what lessons these precedents reveal, the Urban Land Institute undertook for the FHA a study of some 349 homeowners associations. The study, to be published this spring, is highly encouraging. On the whole, the study reports, the associations have worked quite well and there has been a high degree of satisfaction with them on the part of the homeowners, developers and public officials. (The report will be available at $10.00 from the Urban Land Institute, 1200 18th Street, N.W., Washington, D.C. 20036.)

Several principles, however, are indispensable for success. As the model forms in Appendix C demonstrate, there can be considerable variation in the articles of incorporation, covenants, deed forms and such. It is the common denominators that are important. There are six of them:

1. The homeowners association must be set up before the houses are sold.

2. Membership must be mandatory for each home buyer, and any successive buyer.

3. The open space restrictions must be permanent, not just for a given period of years.

4. The association must be responsible for liability insurance, local taxes, and the maintenance of recreational and other facilities.

5. Homeowners must pay their pro rata share of the cost and the assessment levied by the association can become a lien on the property.

6. The association must be able to adjust the assessment to meet changed needs.

Let us now follow the history of the typical cluster development and see how this works out in practice. The first step is for the developer to declare what he is going to do. In order to get approval from the planning commission he files a declaration of covenants and restrictions. These will include the ones that are usually standard for any kind of subdivision — homes to be used only for residential purposes, no livestock around, etc. In the case of a cluster subdivision the developer will also declare what open space is to be deeded to the residents, and what recreational and other facilities he binds himself to provide. He will stipulate that a homeowners association is to be set up and that the open space will be deeded to it.

All buyers must be members. The deed form for each will state that the purchaser is getting ownership of his particular lot and in addition rights and obligations in ʰhe homeowners association.

How early should the association be set up? Some developers believe it best to defer such decision until homes are up and sold. If they do wait, they will generally bind themselves to provide the necesary facilities

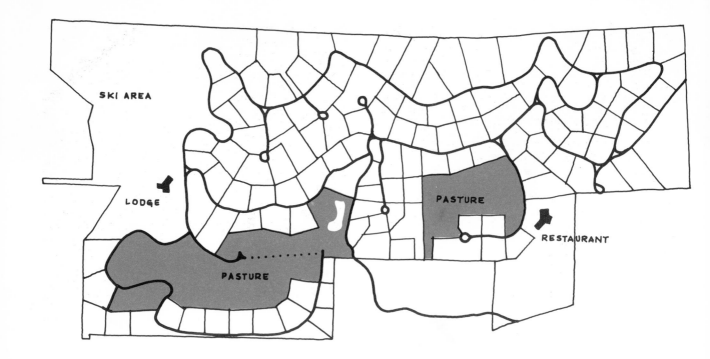

Common areas are usually park and recreation sites but other uses—such as farming—can be as enhancing. At Starwood, a 900 acre lot sale development outside Aspen, Colorado, planners Harman, O'Donnell and Henninger laid out the bulk of the home sites on the slopes, and saved 300 acres of the meadows below as common area. Homeowners association will lease it as pasture land; cattle will provide the pastoral scene and with no charge for maintenance.

and to operate them until there is an association. To cover the costs in the meantime they will make a direct levy or add a sum to the fee to be paid at closing. In any event, the initiative for establishing the association must come from the developer.

Why not just leave it up to the homeowners? This sounds like the democratic thing to do but trouble is apt to result. In a letter to homeowners the developers of The Highlands in Ledyard, Connecticut give a good explanation:

As our post card to you of January 7th indicated, we have been working for well over a year to develop a charter and by-laws for a social association for The Highlands. It is not our intention to usurp your prerogative as homeowners to act to form an association. However, to be realistically workable from your standpoint and ours, this association should be formed in a special manner, and because of past experience we are in the best position to provide the necessary guiding force.

In prior Lifetime subdivisions, several shortcomings have always occurred with association formation. (a) The residents, because of lack of experience, have required a long series of lengthy meetings to get a fundamental organizational structure worked out — rules, objectives, etc. — all of which has resulted in much arguing and bickering. (b) Undue legal expenses were always incurred. (c) Residents' enthusiasm started out very high, as much as 80%, and gradually dwindling down to as low as 10%. (d) Most residents adopted the attitude that they could not be deprived of the benefits of community land or real estate by reason of not joining, so why should they incur the liability of joining. Hence, whatever poor maintenance program has been left, has been paid for by the minority, and has been unsatisfactory at best.

The letter goes on to explain how the association would work, and encloses a proposed charter and set of by-laws. (See Appendix D1).

THE best course, experience suggests, is to set up the association at the very beginning. Along with the covenants and model deed the developer supplies the articles of incorporation of the association and a full set of by-laws. These will provide for equal representation—one lot, one vote—and give the standard procedures for meetings, quorums, and the like.

At McDougal Gardens, a block of old houses in Greenwich Village, portions of back lots were pooled to make a commons.

Extensive open space network of Radburn has been maintained by a homeowners association since 1930.

There are as yet no homeowners. The developer owns everything and thus the officers of the association will often turn out to be his brother-in-law, secretary, or associates. There is a provision, however, insuring that control will be transferred to homeowners. This is virtually automatic: as the ownership of the lots passes from developer to homeowners, so, proportionately, does the control. For good measure, however, there may be a clause stating that when 51% of the lots are sold there may be a special meeting of the membership.

The association will be responsible for maintaining liability insurance on the common areas, paying local taxes on the property, and for maintaining the area and operating its recreational and other facilities. Assessments to pay for this are usually levied once a month. Generally, the assessment will consist of the operating cost divided by the number of homes, though in some cases there will be a formula for scaling the payment according to the size of the house — so much for a two-bedroom house, so much for a three-bedroom. The assessment will be binding and if the homeowner welshes on his payment, the delinquent payment becomes a lien on the property and the association is required to enforce it.

On the average, monthly assessments run between $20 to $30. Where services are elaborate, of course, the charge can run considerably higher; when parking service, exterior maintenance, gatehouses and the like are thrown in, the charge will be as high as $40. Cooperatives and condominiums tend to offer a rather wide range of services and though the cost may not be separated out of the overall monthly charge, it can amount to quite a chunk.

Whatever the sum, a specific dollar figure should not be frozen into the legal agreements. Initially, for example, $10 a month might cover the facilities provided in the first phase of the development, but be quite inadequate when facilities are later expanded. Homeowners should clearly understand that assessments must be adjusted to meet changing needs. At the same time, they have a right to know what they are getting in for, so the articles may set a provisional maximum and provide that it can be increased only by majority vote of the membership or a 2/3 vote. There should also be a provision enabling the association to levy special assessments for capital expenditures, such as the construction of an additional swimming pool.

How big will the tax load be? This depends largely on who the assessor is. If he's like most of them, he will set a very low assessed value on the common open space. Golf courses may be another matter but most assessors try to keep an open space valuation on the course itself rather than compute it on the basis of what it would fetch on the open market.

Legally, the question of open space assessment depends to a large extent on what guarantees there are that it will remain open. If there are none, the assessor can properly figure the valuation on the basis of its development potential. Most assessors don't do this even when there are no guarantees, but they could if they wanted to; indeed, they would have to if they hewed strictly to the law. Ultimately, then, assurance

Interior court at Sunnyside Gardens.

of low assessment on common open spaces rests on the assurance that they won't be developed.

THIS brings us to another question. There are guarantees that the developer will carry out his part of the bargain. But what about the association? Could not the members later decide to make a pretty penny by selling the common property for development? This possibility worries a good many people and is often cited as a compelling reason for demanding municipal ownership.

But the question can be asked in the other direction too. In actual practice, the danger that the homeowners will fill in the common areas is considerably less real than the danger that municipal officials may eventually decide to use the open space for a town parking lot or a sewage disposal plant. (In the deed of Village Green's common open space to Hillsborough, N. J., the only strings are that it be for public purposes.)

It would be very difficult for a homeowners association to convert the open space. In the first place, a majority of the owners would have to agree to it; to date there has been no known instance of such a sell-out. Second, even if they did agree, the space couldn't be developed without a major zoning change. The local government made the common space a condition of approving the original plan; there would have to be an extraordinary new set of circumstances to justify a change.

It should be reiterated, however, that all this rests on a clear and permanent ownership arrangement for the open spaces. The case of Sunnyside Gardens, is instructive. Forty years ago, when this early prototype of the garden city was being developed in Queens, it was decided that the interior commons would consist of portions of the individually owned lots, but all owners would be given access easements to use this space. This system, also used in McDougal Gardens in Greenwich Village, has worked quite satisfactorily.

But there was one rub. The Sunnyside easements, instead of being in perpetuity, were for forty years. They are now expiring. Most of the people want to continue the commons but a few have thought of fencing off their part or putting up a garage on it. On the basis of recent meetings it now appears that the various block groups will be able to extend the easements—this time for perpetuity, and revocable only by a vote of two-thirds of the owners. But it's learning the hard way.

If the original deeds are tightly drawn, there is little danger that a homeowners association will give up its open space. But it doesn't have to be left at that. Legally, there is a further clincher. When the developer is filing his covenants the local government can require an open space easement on the common area. The common area will still be deeded to the homeowners association, and the easement will not give the general public the right of access. The public's interest is, simply, that the open space remain open, and this is is what the easement provides. Local governments in California have favored this method; among others, Monterey County and the city of Fremont (see Appendix D) require such easements as standard operating procedure in approving subdivisions, and such a stipulation is a part of the new cluster regulations proposed by Santa Clara County.

All these various deeds and covenants add up to a hefty pile of documents and they're not the most exciting reading. Nevertheless, it's important to have such a packet for prospective buyers. The substance can be easily explained to them and though they may not read a word of the fine print, this is partly because it's there to read if they want to. They grasp the main point quite readily: the documents are not only an earnest of good faith by the developer; they are a certification by the local government that a binding compact has been made.

Chapter VII

TOWN HOUSE DEVELOPMENTS

IN these next two chapters we will take up individual developments one by one; first, town house developments; next, detached house developments and "super" developments. Since all the vital statistics are collated in the Appendix, we will touch only on those features of these particular developments that seem noteworthy. Where we think a development is unusually good in some respect, or poor, we say so. But no qualitative judgement is implied by the order of listing or the space allotted. The order of listing will be, roughly, from north to south and east to west.

Morrell Park

Philadelphia, where the row house is a venerable institution, is a good place to start, for it has produced what may be the most significant large-scale project in the country—significant not only for the good things about it, but for a few things not so good. It is hard to think of an experiment that may yield so many lessons per acre.

It came about when Edmund Bacon, Philadelphia's spirited planning director, and his associates pondered the fate of the undeveloped farm land that remained in the Far Northeast section of the city. Before long, the way things were going, the area would be chopped up by a host of small developments, none of them much to look at and with a crazy-quilt street pattern that would be difficult for the city to service.

The planners decided that the city would lay down the master subdivision plan and incorporate in it all of the principles they had long been advocating. It was to be a cluster layout, with the 5,000 acre tract divided into a series of neighborhoods. Within this pattern developers could build to their own taste, but the pattern was so strongly outlined that the end result would be the kind of unity that ordinarily is possible only when one large developer is doing the whole thing.

In laying down the open spaces to be dedicated, the planners capitalized on the natural network of wooded streams that lace the area. Instead of an aggregation of bits and pieces, accordingly, the separate portions will be linked into a unified whole; not only functional for recreation, they at once define the neighborhoods and connect them. So far, 350 acres have been dedicated, with a market value of roughly $1 million.

Within the developed areas, the row house is the basic unit. Customarily builders have been putting these up in long rectangular blocks, with a concrete alleyway up the middle. The Far Northeast plan specified that there could not be more than ten units in a row, and it called for grouping the units in essentially circular patterns. Garages would be on the street side, and the interiors of the clusters would be for the private open spaces.

Builders took to the idea. The master plan went pretty far in telling them what to do, but it provided them excellent densities—about 9 units per acre—and considerable savings in construction over the conventional pattern. Construction of the village here noted, Morrell Park, began in 1959. Other builders have been following suit and the area is now being filled in at a rapid rate, with surprisingly few variations from the original plan. When it is finished it will contain about 17,000 dwelling units and 68,000 people.

In one respect reality has not been as good as intention. Looked at from the air, as the photograph overleaf demonstrates, the curvilinear pattern seems very orderly and pleasing. Looked at from the ground, however, the view is something else again. The order so apparent in aerial perspective disappears. You do not see circles and curves; you see a maze of oblique angles. Buildings seem to go this way and that, and what with the frequent gaps between buildings, you can't be sure you are looking at the backsides or the frontsides.

The trouble seems to be that the buildings do not follow through the logic of the circular pattern. The curves that the planners laid down call for a fresh design, or, if you will, a reworking of older designs, such as crescents and circuses. But the builders put up pretty much the same kind of row house units that they had

From aerial perspective, the curvilinear pattern of Morrell Park has a pleasing symmetry.

been used to. When these are set in a continuous row in rectangular blocks there is monotony, but there is also an order. You know where the blocks begin and end; the backsides are in back, and their impedimenta of wires and gas meters and such don't obtrude. Under the Far Northeast plan, however, the builders have, in effect, taken the row house block, chopped it into segments, and put them in circles and semi-circles. The result is somewhat chaotic.

If there is not to be a jumble, other design elements must be kept clear and consistent. In Morrell Park the street pattern is very well defined and the builders have stuck to a fairly unified treatment of the facades. In some other sections, old subdivision plats and major streets previously laid down forced the planners into more eccentric layouts, and the builders have distracted things further by a confusing variation of facades.

The handling of the private open spaces has been disappointing. For one thing, vestigial front yards are provided for most of the houses. They are too small to be of much use, and yet in the aggregate they take an amount of space that could have been used to better purpose elsewhere. Within the clusters would be one place; the interiors have no common areas within them; only a mess of back yards criss-crossed by laundry lines and fences.

Let us note that the residents are not bothered by the aesthetics or how much better it all might have been. They like the place, very much, and they have good reasons to. At $11,000-$13,000 they get a three-bed-

room house that could not be duplicated for less than $14,000 in adjoining areas. Sales have been excellent, and the people who have been there some time seem well satisfied with the house and with the way the neighborhood is shaking down.

When residents praise the neighborhood, they talk about its safety, its quiet streets, its good transportation and its convenient shopping centers. They do not, interestingly, talk about the open space network or the recreation potential of the area. Salesmen in the model houses report that prospective buyers rarely ask a question about these features.

It is apparent that the small backyard is the open space residents care about, and for those who have come from the central city it is a fine space indeed. Residents use these yards and they like them. They mention how excellent they are for raising children, and how nice it is to have a yard for play equipment.

But it is the public open space that is the unique feature of the Far Northeast, and it would seem that residents could hardly help being impressed. There is so much of it—more than later residents will have, for some of the space is land that will be developed later. But for the moment, at least, the community open spaces don't mean much to the residents, and to a few they are a downright danger. (When asked about a nearby stream, one mother quickly volunteered that she certainly wouldn't let her children play there; she realized the danger.)

Philadelphia's master plan for the Far Northeast area.

Interior spaces at Morrell Park from eye and balcony level.

One reason for the keen interest is that not much has been done yet by the various city departments to landscape the network or develop recreation facilities; there is one very handsome green, but most of the common sites are apt to be littered and the streams are polluted. But just as important a factor, perhaps, is the background of the new residents. They are city people, and it's understandable that they don't easily visualize using streamside walkways and bridle trails and such. They've never known them.

Most of their children haven't either, but they are learning. Philadelphia has a notably progressive recreation department, and director Robert Crawford feels that one of the big challenges is how to educate city people to enjoy such an environment, and not merely its formal, supervised activities. There will be a fairly elaborate program to develop recreational facilities such as skating rinks, baseball diamonds and tennis courts, but one of the best features of the open space plan is that many parts of the wooded area are to be left as is —for children to explore on their own and with no one around to blow the whistle.

Paradoxically, as subsequent development diminishes the total amount of open space, the residents, adults as well as children, may come to appreciate the open space network much more than at present. The continuity that it provides is the less obvious now for there being so many other spaces, but as these fill up what remains may

then seem the dearer and the more inviting. Whatever the result, the Far Northeast should provide a fascinating case study in the response of city people to such an environment.

Future creek valley greenway.

PHILADELPHIA TOWN HOUSES

Close to the center of town, Philadelphia boasts some very handsome town house projects. In the Society Hill redevelopment area are the town houses and tower designed by Oskar Stonorov (upper left), and the Alcoa complex designed by I. M. Pei (bottom). About 40 blocks west on Spruce is University Mews, by Ronald Turner (upper right). None are corned up with trick variations. In common, they have facades of classic simplicity and their interior open spaces, like Pei's (left), are done as formal courts.

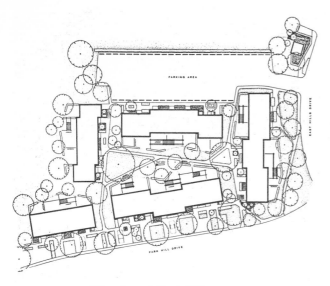

Site plan of East Hills court.

Interior commons.

East Hills Park

The potential of cluster to help fill the middle income housing gap is well illustrated by East Hills Park in Pittsburgh. It is the result of an unusual civic effort. Sparked by Richard K. Mellon, Pittsburgh leaders created a non-profit development fund, Action Housing, Inc.— a sort of private development authority, the idea of which was to back first-rate projects by private developers by lending them money at 6% for most of the cost (90% of the land cost, 70% of the construction cost.) In addition to supplying the money, this powerful civic group also provided a strong assist in getting the necessary zoning changes made to permit cluster development.

Labor made quite a contribution, too. For one thing, the building trade unions decided to use their pension fund to supply mortgage money; as a result the mortgage rate is 4¾%, which per month means a saving to the home buyer of about $7.50. For the first project, East Hills Park, the building trades also worked out a unique contract with the builder Roland Catarinella; it provides that there will be no work stoppages over jurisdictional squabbles, and it frees the builder to use new labor-saving techniques.

The design history has been a trifle complicated. With considerable fanfare, Action Housing retained José Sert, Walter Gropius and Carl Koch to do the initial plans and subsequently staged a big clinic for a critique of them. For the final patterns, however, builder Caterinella brought in Nicholas Satterlee and Kenneth Johnstone. Under the pressure to get the thing going a number of innovations and features of the preliminary concept had to be dropped, but the result is a pleasing layout.

The original aim of providing a good house at a price middle income families can afford has certainly been realized. A two-bedroom unit, complete with all the usual extras such as disposals and gas-fired incinerators, sells for $12,350. The financing is excellent. It can be bought for $400 down and a monthly payment, including taxes and insurance, comes to only $81. Except for utilities, the only extra is $8 for common maintenance and this includes not only the care of the open spaces but all exterior painting and roof repair.

But the houses do need selling. As other projects have demonstrated, the price appeal can be considerably offset by local partiality against row housing and the lack of garages. The question of how much integration there will be can also be a troublesome factor. Sales, as a consequence, have been nothing to shout about. But of the 110 houses that have been finished, 70 have been occupied. Three hundred units in all, including some garden apartments, have been planned for phase one. The eventual goal is for some 3,000 units, but no firm plans will be drawn up for it until phase one is digested.

Capitol Park

We come now to several very interesting redevelopment projects. Ordinarily, the term "redevelopment project" would tell you what they looked like: a group of towers placed on a mall, in a design of overpowering dullness. There are exceptions, and here, cheek by jowl in Washington's southwest redevelopment area, are two of the best. Both mix town houses and towers; both provide usable open spaces, private and public. They are good looking and people like them.

Capitol Park tower and town house units.

Trees and passageway give nice enclosure.

The first, Capitol Park, was sponsored by redevelopers Roger Stevens and James Scheuer. For the 30 acre tract architect Chlothiel Smith designed a complex of 400 town houses and five high rise towers. The first section was finished and occupied for two years; the rest is under construction and should be completed in early 1964. Rentals are by no means inexpensive—$180 to $200 a month for two-bedroom town houses—but all the completed town houses are filled up, and so are the towers.

If one adjective had to be selected to describe the overall effect, it would be "pleasant." The towers and the town houses set each other off quite well, and the open spaces are highly functional. There is one largish open space, but at a human scale, and functional; it has a reflecting pool and a covered pavilion which, with a handsome barbecue hearth, is meant to be used and is.

The relationship between some of the small garden spaces adjoining the town houses and the larger public open spaces is not completely satisfactory—in some cases the two tend to merge, with little visible separation, and privacy suffers. On the whole, however, the private spaces seem well used and enjoyed. Charcoal grills are all over the place, and if some of the garden areas are a bit cluttered, it is a genial clutter of velocipedes and outdoor furniture. Children abound.

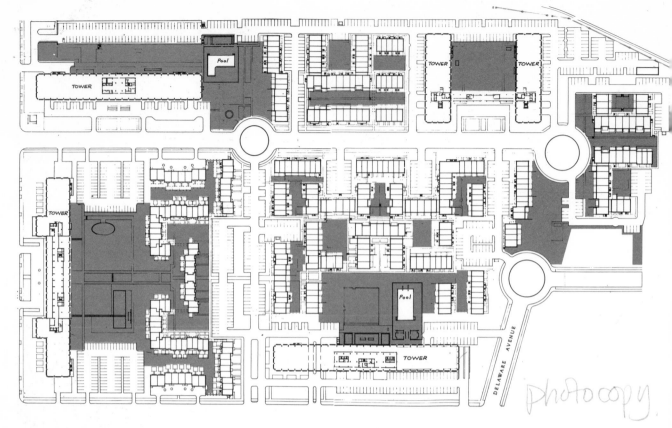

Site plan of Capitol Park.

River Park

A few blocks south is River Park. It, too, combines town houses and towers, but with quite a different approach. The word here is "striking." For the Reynolds Metals Company, sponsor of the project, architect Charles Goodman designed a large tower with a foreground of town houses. The town houses are something of a composition; with their mixture of flat roofs and barrel vault roofs set off with different primary colors, they provide from a number of angles views with the fascination of a puzzle. Visually, River Park is a knockout.

Here the emphasis is on privacy. There is very little green; the common areas are paved and they function primarily as walkways. Between these and the patios there is no ambiguity whatsoever. The walls surrounding the individual patios are seven feet high, and it is impossible for the passerby to see what's going on inside. The people in the towers can, of course, but the possibility doesn't seem to have been inhibiting.

It certainly didn't dampen the interest of purchasers. River Park's units are cooperatives and their price ranges from $22,000 for a two-story town house to $31,550 for a three-story one. All were sold out before construc-

tion was completed and no model house ever had to be operated. The tower units went more slowly, but by fall 1963 virtually all units were sold.

Layout of River Park.

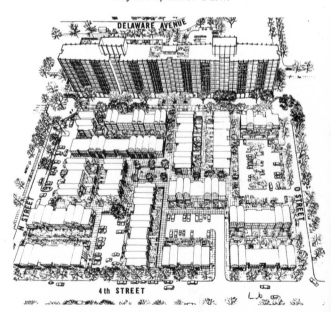

Capitol Park private and common areas blend.

River Park private spaces are sharply separated.

Formal court is focal point for River Park town houses.

Georgetown South

Town houses may go well in town, many people argue, but could they ever really catch on in suburbia? And would they go over with the middle income group? Thirty miles south of River Park an important market test has been taking place. For some time Merit Developers, Inc. wanted to try a town house and village green project in the suburbs of Washington. Under the zoning of most adjacent Virginia counties, town houses could be constructed only if they were rental units, so the developers pushed on to Prince William County. This was stretching the limit of commutation pretty far, but the local authorities eventually proved willing to revise their ordinances to allow the building of a town house cluster development.

The result is a clean, economic layout. Architect Marion Bagley has laid out the houses in straight rows, with the rows grouped to make a series of blocks, each with its own common green in the center. The developers did not provide the customary swimming pools, only sites, but they have dressed up the greens with barbecue pits, swings, and play equipment, and they merchandise the package very effectively. Common areas will be deeded to a homeowners association; pending its formation each home is assessed $3 a month for maintenance.

There is a nod to the suburban front yard (though setbacks were reduced to fifteen feet from the previously required thirty-five), but in other respects the design salutes the city as its inspiration, especially Georgetown, Alexandria, and Williamsburg. The street scenes have been carefully composed for this effect, with some thirty-five basic exteriors used to give variation.

It may not be Georgetown, but at $11,490 to $14,990 a house, it is quite a sales package. Construction began in January 1963. By June, 170 houses had been sold; by December, 205. Most of the buyers have been people

Typical Georgetown South block.

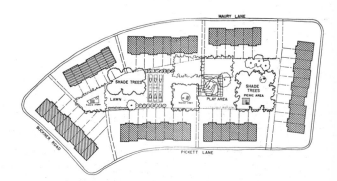

Commons are well merchandised. This is the scene at the rear of the model houses.

50

Landscaping plan for Georgetown South saves best trees.

who work in Washington, with government workers the biggest single group. It's a big market to tap, and the chances of selling out the total 900 units planned seem rather good.

Colonial Park

A development that has had a highly catalytic effect, particularly in spurring suburban cluster subdivisions, is Colonial Park in Louisville. It is a low-cost redevelopment project for negroes.

When proposals were invited for the redevelopment of the Southwick area in Louisville, the usual barracks layouts were drawn up. Local builders Bollinger and Martin, however, wanted to try a cluster town house design, and at the Louisville Home Show in March 1960 demonstrated what it could look like. Many people thought it would be a very refreshing change; it was so economical in layout, furthermore, that the houses could be priced at between $8,500 and $12,000.

Official response was mixed. The zoning ordinance would allow town houses only as rental units, and the planning and zoning commission recoiled at the thought of a change. The City Works Director was especially strong in opposition; these were *row* houses, he main-

tained, and to open the gates to them would lead to slum building. If they were to get going, Bollinger and Martin would have to start the project as a rental one.

Most of the county's planning staff and the local federal housing people, however, were strong for the cluster idea, and they got together to draft a new ordinance. They also worked with the builders to draw up a model homes association setup. Louisville also had on the premises one of the country's leading architectural journalists, the *Courier Journal's* Grady Clay, and the citizenry as a result was given a first rate and continuous education on the need for a new approach.

The NAHB, recognizing this was a crucial test, helped out with a formidable array of promotional material. *House and Home* Magazine scheduled a highly favorable article on the development, and on the day of the hearings on the new ordinance, Bollinger and Martin distributed advance proofs of the article. By this time, the city powers had been pretty well sold. On January 30, 1961 the new regulations were approved. Principally, they provided that the houses could be built for sale if they had a minimum width of 18 ft. and an average lot size area of at least 2,400 square feet.

Bollinger and Martin now began building the rest of

Court units at Colonial Park (taken early 1963).

the project on a for-sale basis. Plans called for 480 units, with the houses grouped 3 to 14 units in each row, with the rows to be set around small commons, these connected to each other by walks. Each house would have a small front yard, fenced back yards. Group parking areas adjoined the commons. Eventually a swimming pool and club house would be built. The average house, on a lot 18 feet wide, was priced at $10,000, or, to put it more accurately, $63 per month.

Less than 24 hours after the *House and Home* April issue appeared, scores of housing professionals began telephoning, telegraphing and writing Messrs. Bollinger and Martin; more than 400 made trips to Louisville to have a look at the project. Many brought their sketch books with them, and almost identical designs have since been projected in a number of cities. The architects of the project, Augustus and Doumas, sold similar plans to 20 builders.

The sales response was phenomenal. By spring of 1962 there were over 500 sales. There was one flaw, however. The lower income people in the area were willing enough to buy the houses; the trouble was, they couldn't pay for them. So far, only one out of every ten persons who signed up for a house has been able to qualify financially for a mortgage. At this rate, Bollinger and Martin would have to close 4,000 sales to get 400 that could satisfy the FHA credit standards, and that, as Mr. Bollinger says, is no way to make money.

Ironically, the builders are now trying to convert the rest of the project to a rental basis. They are closing out the homes for sale at 104 units. For the remaining 376 units to be built, they are trying to get approval of a new financing scheme under which they would build the units for a non-profit corporation which in turn would rent them. Under Section 221-d-3, the government would arrange a loan at 3⅛ per cent. This would enable the corporation to set the rents as low as $59 per month and there certainly is a market at this scale.

Despite the financing difficulties, the project has cinched the cluster idea for the Louisville area. The impact has been strongest on suburbia. Most of the builders are now energetically looking for suitable sites in outlying areas; another cluster project, Heather Hills, is already opened up and several more are in the early construction phase.

Miller, Wihry and Brooks, the landscape architects who had drafted the Colonial Park site plan, were commissioned to apply the cluster principle to two quite large projects in the suburbs of Louisville, both well up the income scale. (One of them, Hunting Creek, is discussed in the next chapter.)

Hartshorn

Very similar to Colonial Park is a town house project, Hartshorn, in Richmond, Virginia. It, too, is in a redevelopment area and is a predominantly negro project. The site plan groups units around a series of common greens, as at Colonial Park; the houses are in the same price range and they tap the same kind of market.

But in this instance sales were slow. It was completed in June of 1962, but a year later 28 homes were still unsold. The last units were closed out in the fall of 1963. Richmond's redevelopment authority feels the houses are an extraordinarily fine value, but they note that a number of factors were working against a good sales record in this instance.

The neighborhood is a blighted one and the negro home buyers of the area have had a strong desire to move into single family homes. There was also an unfortunate changeover in sales personnel. But while it took a good bit of time to get people to buy, those who have bought have taken great pride in their homes and the garden areas, and a fairly active community life has been developing.

Plan of main block at Hartshorn.

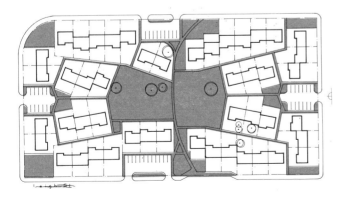

Dudley Square townhouses.

Dudley Square

Another Georgetown type development, but at the upper end of the price scale, is Dudley Square, in Shreveport, Louisiana. Real estate man N. O. Thomas had long hankered to try a town house project, and when he acquired an irregular tract bordering a drainage canal he asked architects Somdal, Smitherman and Sorenson to see what they could do with it.

The prevailing zoning called for 6,000 square foot minimum lots. The architects' plan took the 20 houses the acreage would allow, squeezed the lot sizes down to 1,300-1,500 square feet, and massed the space left over for a common. It was a handsome design, and the city approved.

The result is an enclave, with a notable emphasis on privacy. Each of the houses has its own walled garden, and the common green they front upon is itself enclosed by a brick wall. There is only one entry, and that is guarded by a gate. Prices were similarly exclusive: beginning at $35,000 (24 foot wide model) up to $55,000 (36 feet wide). Fourteen sold before construction began, the remainder by the end of the year.

Dudley Square site plan.

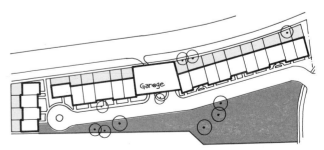

The green at Dudley Square.

Each homeowner has a one-twentieth interest in the commons and is a member of the Dudley Square corporation. This provides, at a charge of about $40 a month, a full range of services: among other things, a full time landscape gardener, janitor service, and for the garage, which is done up as a Georgian stable, an attendant on duty all 24 hours. There are also those gas lamps.

Most of the people who can afford such houses have already raised their children, so no recreational facilities for youngsters have been provided. But it is useful for them just the same. Mr. Thomas, who lives in Dudley Square himself, notes that the green seems to be full of grandchildren on the weekends and may have some pulling power in getting married sons and daughters to come and visit.

Geneva Terrace

When Eichler Homes, Inc., perhaps the West Coast's leading builder of upper income subdivisions, decided to do a cluster project it went all the way, and the result, Geneva Terrace, is as pure an example of cluster as you will find anywhere. Aesthetically, it demonstrates that a house design which doesn't try for facade variation can be quite stunning. Architect Claude Oakland's houses are identical, but the rows are not long and they do not give the effect of monotony at all, and though the brick fronts and arched windows are almost classically simple, the overall effect has a good bit of warmth.

The design is also notable as an exercise in space economics. It had to be. The site, on the southern boundary of the city, cost $86,000 per acre for the 21½ acres, and Eichler had to cost out the project so that the houses could start under $30,000. There is hardly a square foot of wasted space. Most notable is the handling of parking; the design separates the parking areas from the houses and groups them in partially covered courts; this saves curb cuts and it enables more of the available open space to be massed for the commons. These are fairly tight, but they are just large enough to give a reasonable feeling of expanse. The project, the first to be constructed under San Francisco's new planned unit development ordinance (see Appendix C) also calls for two tower units at one corner of the site. Eichler will get around to these when he is over the hump on the town houses.

This will take some time, for sales have been slow. The problem is the neighborhood. A public housing project is near the site, and in general the area is rather nondescript. It is being upgraded but, as with several projects in other cities, it takes a bit of imagination to visualize how good it could be, and for the time being the neighborhood and the level of the house prices, $28,000, are out of whack.

But the potential market to be tapped could be quite large. Most of the buyers so far are city apartment dwellers who have wanted to house their growing family in the city but have been unable to afford the cost of a move

54

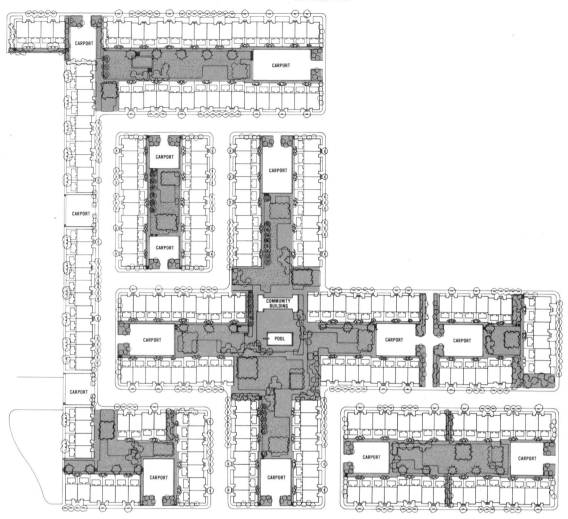

Geneva Terrace site plan; area at upper right is reserved for high rise units.

Use of group carports at Geneva Terrace provides more space for interior commons.

Brick fronts of Geneva Terrace town houses are clean, identical, and handsome.

to the usual apartment towers. It is a cosmopolitan group; there is a considerable proportion of professional people among the first buyers, and a number of negro and oriental families.

Pomeroy Green

For a second cluster project, Eichler went down the peninsula to the suburb of Santa Clara. It is a smaller project with 78 units on seven and a half acres. The density is the same as Geneva Terrace—10 units to the acre—and again Claude Oakland's layout is clean and tight. In one spot it seems a bit too tight. There is not much space between the pool and surrounding houses; since there are many children at Pomeroy Green things can get a bit noisy of an afternoon.

Unlike Geneva Terrace, there are individual parking garages rather than the more space saving carport areas. Eichler doesn't feel that suburbia is ready yet for such an innovation, though he hopes the day will come.

At the time Pomeroy Green was being sold, Eichler was merchandising several conventional subdivisions in the same area. When the salesmen checked with each

Interior of a Geneva Terrace block.

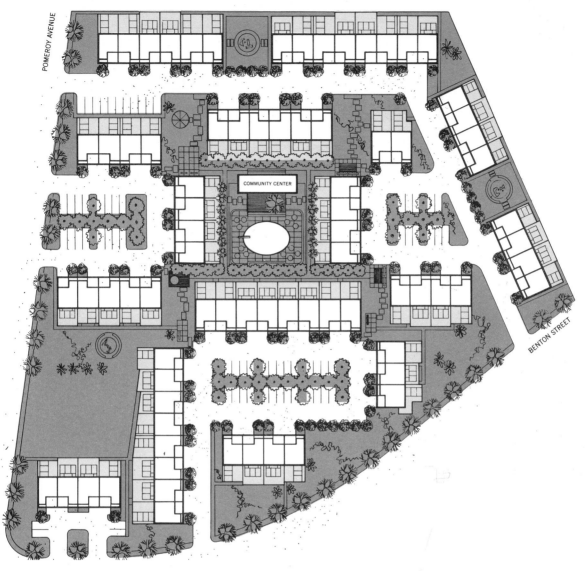

POMEROY AVENUE

COMMUNITY CENTER

BENTON STREET

Plan of Pomeroy Green.

Pool area is the epicenter.

other on the prospects they found that contrary to usual experience there was not much duplication among the people who came to look at the model houses. Those who were attracted to Pomeroy Green tended to be people who had been living in the area, many of them in detached houses. The people who showed a partiality for Eichler's conventional subdivisions, by contrast, tended to be people just moving into the area.

Sales were a bit slow at Pomeroy Green, but eventually all units were sold and the whole project worked well enough to encourage Eichler to start another one, Pomeroy West, on an adjacent tract. It is quite similar, but here Eichler is introducing a variation in the form of an atrium house.

Each Creekside court has its own pool.

Creekside

This condominium project, located in Walnut Creek, California, is a superb job of tight site planning—and probably the best example in the country of skillful enclosure. Architect Larry Freels grouped his two-story units to create a series of quite intimate common spaces. They could seem cramped, but on the ground they do not. For one thing, they are almost totally enclosed; second, excellent use has been made of the existing trees; third, the architectural treatment contributes to the enclosure by such features as an open stairway and a covered entry.

Each small commons, furthermore, has its own swimming pool. As the site plan at upper right shows, Creekside is unusually generous in this respect; the trend elsewhere, however, seems to be in the same direction. From a purely recreation viewpoint, it could be more economic to build one or two large pools, but when the pools are an integral landscape and architectural feature, the cost accounting works out well. Lawns don't cost a great deal less, nor would their maintenance. Furthermore, when a project is built in stages, as was Creekside, good merchandising strategy dictates that each section be

reasonably complete, and with its own pool. The nearer to the pool, the quicker a unit sells. If there was to be only one large pool for the whole project, it would have

Fences emphasize privacy.

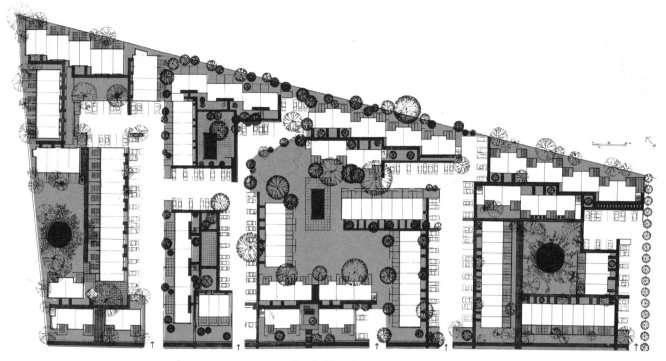

Creekside plan.

Rheem Terrace.

to be built along with the first section and the amount of financing required for it would be disproportionate. It is true that one pool is easier to supervise than several but this is a problem chiefly when there are many children about; in this case very few of the residents are young couples with children.

Even were there more open space to play around with, Freels would not want to make his interior open spaces appreciably larger. He is against big areas; after observing a number of large projects, such as Baldwin Hills, he has come to the conclusion that people do not use their big spaces very much because the scale is wrong. It is the more intimate spaces they use most.

Nor need privacy suffer in the smaller spaces. Each Creekside unit has either an enclosed ground floor patio or a second floor balcony. The people who live in the balcony units can peer down at the patio if they are so disposed; the angles are such, however, that the patio is effectively in defilade.

A second condominium project by the same builder and architect is Rheem Terrace in nearby Rheem Valley (right). Because of the drawing power of the poolside units at Walnut Creek, Rheem Terrace has as many units as possible around the pool. The site lacks the trees of Creekside but it is on a hillside and the layout makes a very pleasing use of the changes in grade.

Rheem Terrace.

Peacock Gap houses face out on golf course.

The Terrace at Peacock Gap

The sybaritic effect which Californians carry off so well is also evident in this unusual town house project. It is a unit of a much larger development, Marin Bay, which has been planned for a 2,233 acre peninsula at the northern end of San Francisco Bay. Eventually it is to include a mixture of housing types and such features as a resort hotel, yacht club and a group of luxury restaurants. The first phase of the development, chiefly lot sales, has taken place in a natural basin the floor of which has been made into a golf course, with the houses on the slopes surrounding it.

The town house project, sponsored by US Plywood and designed by architect Sherrill Broudy, has a site of only 1½ acres (raw land cost—$50,000 an acre). By borrowing space from the golf course, however, this combination of small private spaces and common pool area manages to convey a considerable feeling of openness. The 16 houses are laid out in an arc. Parking is on the street side and entry is made into small atriums. On the other side are private terraces facing out on the swimming pool area and golf course. The houses were sold on a condiminium basis at $25,000 to $30,000. Complete exterior maintenance is provided for by the homeowners association. Monthly charge: $39. US Plywood and Broudy have collaborated on a similar project, Crystal Shores, at Lake Tahoe.

Because of the expanse beyond, Peacock Gap plan gets maximum effect from small common area.

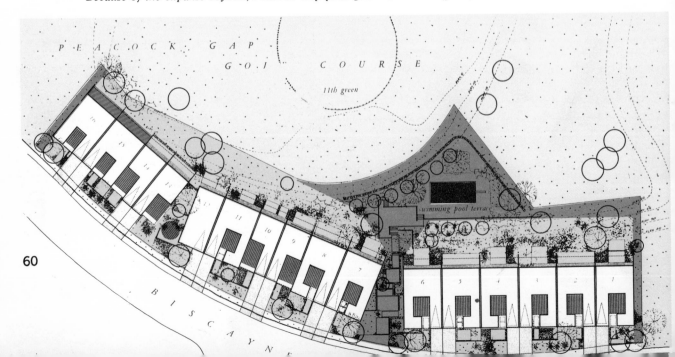

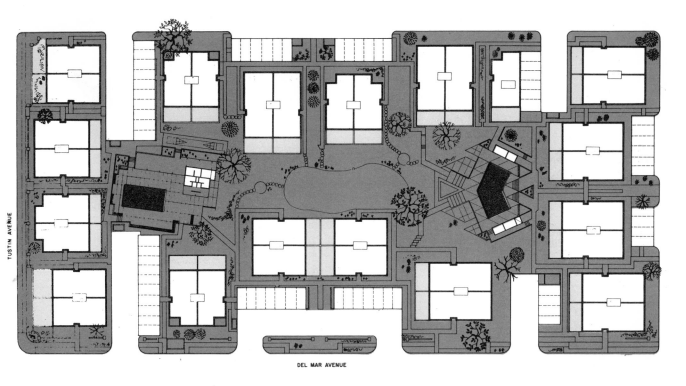

Vista Bahia site plan.

Vista Bahia

A project which has led to several important precedents started three and a half years ago when Resplan Inc., a group of real estate men, bought a 5 acre tract in Newport Beach, California. It was high cost land—$30,000 an acre—and to develop it they wanted not only to use the cluster principle but to set up the development as a condominium.

Neither feature was provided for in Newport Beach's statutes. The city officials were hospitable to the cluster idea but thought that the development should be a co-operative rather than a condominium. Over the next eighteen months the realtors and the city officials worked together on drafting new enabling ordinances. The realtors' case for the condominium approach stressed the point that the individual purchaser in a cooperative could lose heavily if the cooperative failed. While they were pressing this case a Newport Beach cooperative did just that. When the new ordinance was finally passed it provided for condominium financing. Because of this and similar efforts elsewhere in California the state legislature in 1963 passed a bill clarifying the tax and financing aspects of condominiums.

Vista Bahia's houses are double houses, done in "French Tahitian" style. There are thirty-three units in all — the same number that could have been put up on larger lots under the previous ordinance. The Vista Bahia plan puts the houses on the periphery, with patios facing inward to the common area. In the middle of this is an eighteen hole putting green. At each end is a swimming pool and bathhouse.

Purchasers acquire the fee to the house and its patio (prices $28,500 to $38,500); all the rest of the area is held in common, including sixty-six garage spaces, two for each homeowner.

Center of area is a putting green.

Here is how they do it in Georgetown itself. These townhouses, laid out in a mews arrangement, were completed in 1959; sold for $60,000 to $85,000.

Chapter VIII

SUPER DEVELOPMENTS

Now going up in the fox hunt country of Fairfax County, Virginia, west of Washington, are the first units of the most ambitious cluster development in the country. Builder Robert Simon of New York proposes to put up an expansive new town that by 1980 will contain some 75,000 people and provide such a variety of housing that it will be a "three-generation" community where people will stay put. No development will be more closely watched by planners; it will be, for one thing, the first example of the kind of satellite community envisioned in Washington's Year 2000 plan. In details as well as general concepts Reston will be a test of a number of interesting propositions.

It starts with the very great advantage of a superb piece of land. The 10½ square mile tract is rolling pasture land and woods, laced with streams, and it is big enough to give site planners the sort of leeway they dream about.

The planners, Whittlesey and Conklin, have done a notable job of tailoring the master plan to the terrain. It is a true cluster plan, with the houses concentrated in seven villages of about 10,000 people each. Most of the intervening woods and meadow land will be left open; there will be five golf courses and two lakes for fishing and boating. One lake already exists; the other was created by throwing a dam across the valley, and it is around this lake that the first village is being built.

The Reston plan pays great respect to the natural drainage network. As noted in Chapter Two, the planners have sought to firm up the creek banks with natural plantings, rather than take the conventional course of lining them with concrete. They didn't win all their creeks — the country engineers insisted on concrete in a number of instances — but most of them remain intact, and very agreeable they are.

For so large an undertaking, Reston bids to be remarkably lacking in the project look. Simon, who has a horror of most housing projects, has been very strong for mixture; there will be a variety of housing types throughout the area, ranging from large lot custom-built homes to a number of town house complexes. Within the complexes themselves there will be considerable variety.

The first village, now going up, has three town house clusters, each done by a different architectural firm — Charles Goodman Associates, Chlothiel Smith, and Whittlesey and Conklin. At one end of the lake will be a village center with an apartment tower and shops.

This is a remarkably tight design for a suburban village, but it has made possible several innovations. One of them is a central water chilling unit for the air conditioning of the town houses. Because of the clustering the pipe runs are short enough to be economic.

In the design of the town houses, as well as in the overall layout, the first village adds up to a very sophisticated design—so sophisticated, indeed, as to pose the question of just how urbane suburbia can be.

The idea of a city in the country has long fascinated planners but no one has really brought it off yet; even the Swedes, with their new town of Vallingby, have found that highly urbane shops and cafes do not take root very well in middle income suburbia.

The Reston effort, however, could very well make its own market. And it is admirably consistent. Without knowing who the architects were, one could grasp very quickly from the designs that they are people who like cities, and the houses should appeal most to people with the same leanings. The concept of the village center also has a certain anti-suburban flavor. The shops are to include the kind of specialty stores found in a place like Georgetown, and the restaurant will not be a Howard Johnson. They hope to get an Italian one.

Another proposition that Reston will explore is the "life cycle" community. Simon hopes that Reston will eventually be not only a residential adjunct to Washington, but a fairly complete city with its own light industry, research parks and such home based cultural attractions as a repertory theatre. At Reston, accordingly, people could find what they wanted at each stage of the cycle and thus there would be far less mobility than is usual in the suburbs.

Model of first village at Reston.

Maybe so, but it's certainly a tough area in which to test the proposition. The income and occupational groups that Reston should draw are by necessity highly mobile, upwards and sideways, and in Washington, D. C., they can be given a further shove by the electorate. There is, of course, quite a pool of stability to be tapped in the civil service; if federal agencies locate offices at Reston, they'll bring along a good core of people who might be glad to stick around.

Much is to be learned, but the plan is flexible and since Reston is being built a phase at a time, advantage can be taken of the lessons as they come. The first village will be especially important to watch. The aim is high—very high—and if the village makes its market, it could raise the sights of developers in many another area.

Crofton

In Maryland, twenty miles east of Washington, another satellite community is being built. The ingredients here are more time tested. The greater part of the 1,600 acre site will be a golf course subdivision, with a 210 acre course surrounded by 2,000 lots. The houses will be detached and the lots will average out to three units to the acre.

The developer, Crawford Corporation of Louisiana, plans to build a town house and apartment section later. The county supervisors are still somewhat leery of town houses, so the developer is trying to get permission to go ahead on a block or two to prove how well it can work out. Another phase of the project calls for an office park, a research park and a large regional shopping center.

Crofton plan puts golf course in middle.

In contrast to Reston's emphasis on the urbane, Crofton's village center will be in small town fashion, with a pleasant arrangement of buildings in Williamsburg style, with bow windows and dormers. There is to be a skating pond in the middle, next to it a teenage soda shop with a canopy terrace warmed by infrared heaters. Social activities will be centered in the Crofton Inn, which will also serve as the club house of the golf course.

Crofton, incidentally, furnishes an interesting example of the workings of the Maryland law for the preferential assessment of farm land. The law provides that land which is being actively farmed should be assessed only on its open space value and with no regard to its sub-division potential. The Crawford Corporation paid somewhere between $2,000 and $2,500 an acre for the land. The site is mostly woodland, but some farming opera-

tions are still being carried on; as a result most portions are being assessed at its open space value, and will continue to be until they are actually built upon.

Americana Fairfax

Steep, wooded sites pose great problems; they also pose great opportunities, and a fine demonstration is builder Carl Freeman's handling of a 260 acre tract in Fairfax County, Virginia.

Freeman wanted to put up a 3,000 unit garden apartment development. At the time he proposed it, Fairfax County had no cluster ordinance, and under the regulations Freeman would have had to spread small units over all the tract, up to a maximum of 20 to the acre. He persuaded the county to set the density on the basis of the total area—and at only 11½ units to the acre.

65

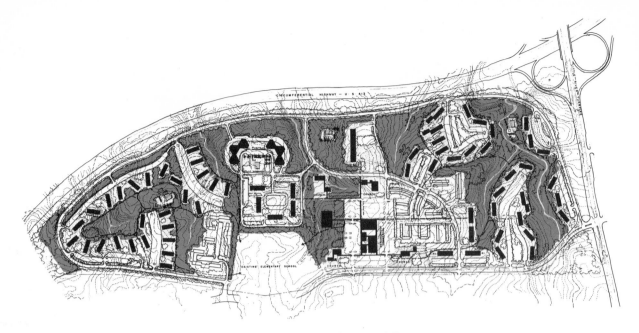

Plan of Americana Fairfax capitalizes on hilliness of tract.

This enabled Freeman to capitalize on the hilliness of the tract rather than cut and fill it away. Much of the housing has been virtually built into the hills—2 stories on the upper side, 4 on the lower. Because of the clustering, the bulk of the area has been left open and most of its magnificent trees left unsawn.

The project is completely rental, but provides a variety of housing types; there are to be 1,800 garden apartments, some 900 medium and high rise units, and 290 town houses. About a third of the units have been completed and all are rented.

Parkwood gives each lot access to common open space.

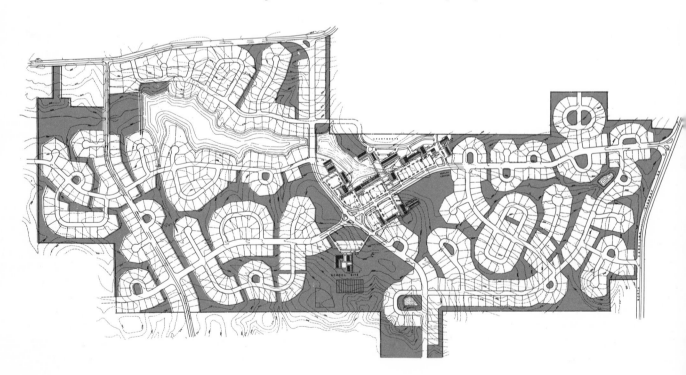

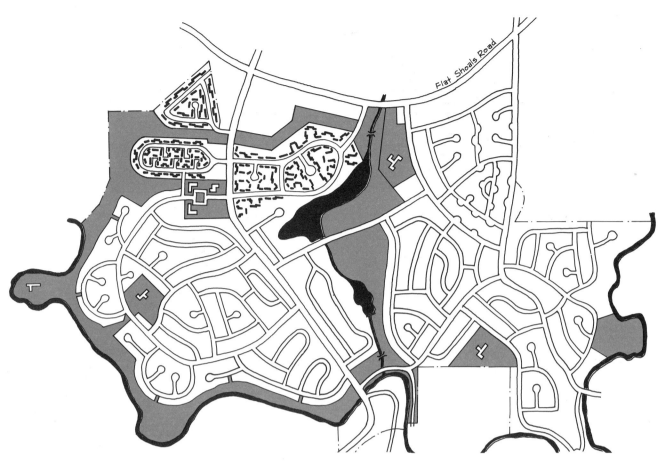

Plan for Chapel Hill

Parkwood

For cluster without tears, a notable example has been going up on a rural 560 acre tract adjoining North Carolina's "Research Triangle" in Durham. Here builder Roger Kavanagh has put up a development that combines standard detached houses with a cluster open space plan. The lots, 750 in all, are set in loops and cul-de-sacs, with each grouping given an open space "eyebrow." The linkage is such that the rear of every lot ties into a continuous open space system.

For a development that has won national recognition —it received the NAHB award for the finest residential community in 1962—Parkwood is remarkable in having roused no local controversy. Kavanagh never used the word cluster and no one feared anything revolutionary was under foot. Zoning wasn't a problem; when Kavanagh said he would put in the water and sewage system himself the county was delighted and permitted him to reduce the regulation lot size 20 to 25%. Market response has been good: all of the 260 houses completed have been sold ($13,000—$22,000) and Kavanagh expects to complete the project by 1966.

Chapel Hill

Gerald Lloyd of New York, a leading advocate of "transferable density," found a good canvas down in the Atlanta area. For a 1,700 acre tract southeast of the city he drew up a cluster plan for a self-contained community, Chapel Hill. Of the 2,900 units provided for, 1,600 will be detached houses. Later there are to be town houses and apartment towers.

Since it is much easier to get approval of the detached house phase of a project, it is a temptation for developers to table the question of subsequent high rise and town house units. The county wasn't enthusiastic about apartments but Lloyd pressed hard, and successfully, for the necessary permission. The initial residents will be owners of single family houses and if the question of apartments was not raised until later, they would very likely feel they were being had and become a formidable opposition.

The open space network will be dedicated to the county, but much landscaping and improvement will be done by the developer. This is a considerable cost item but much of it can be justified as a marketing expense, for the improvement in looks makes lot sales easier.

Plan of village of Bright Coves, New Seabury.

New Seabury

On a 3,000 acre tract of land on the south shore of Cape Cod, developer Emil Hanslin is creating a highly interesting vacation community that could well become an all year one. Lots average 3 to 4 to the acre and are laid out in a cluster plan. There are to be eleven villages, each one with a particular recreational emphasis—one will feature boating, for example; another, surf-fishing. Each of the villages will be separated by swaths of open space or waterways. Only 30% of the site will be used for housing; 59% will be open space; 3% will be devoted to commercial use; 8% to roads.

The first village, Bright Coves, is built around a series of waterways that have been artfully dredged so that each house has a connection with Nantucket Sound. In the summer, water taxis make the regular circuit of all the landings to take residents to the beach club. The water is further merchandised by a string of lamps lining the coves. They are gas street lamps.

A second village, High Wood, is inland, and here Hanslin has featured riding as the motif, with bridle trails through the pine woods and a community stable. As with all the connective open spaces, the land will eventually be owned by a homeowners association.

Sales have been slow. One reason, ironically, lies in the amount of choice afforded by the master plan. The customer not only has a number of excellent model units to choose from—with all sorts of permutations possible, including, of course, a custom-designed house, if he so wishes—he has, in addition, a choice of some eleven environments.

Hanslin now feels that there was too much emphasis on the master plan. The rigors of choice apparently froze many into irresolution, and they reasoned that they would wait until they saw how the other villages shaped up. In his merchandising Hanslin is now emphasizing what they can buy right now.

Hunting Creek

One of the best case histories of the superiority of cluster over conventional is the evolution of the plan of a 964

68

Hunting Creek plan emphasizes natural features the previous plan obliterated.

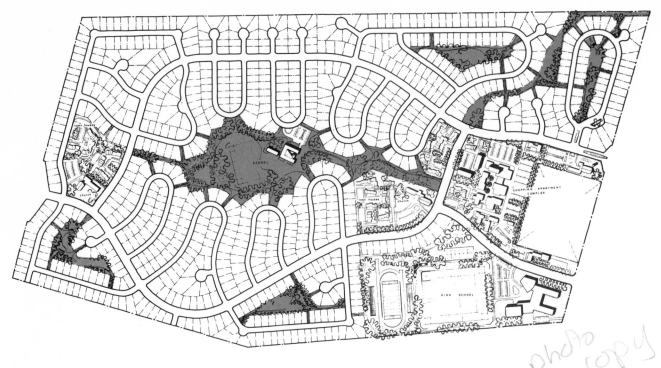

Plan for Westchester uses Radburn superblock as framework.

acre development on the outskirts of Louisville, Kentucky. Back in 1961 the owner of the tract had an engineer draw up a plan that would get as many lots as were legally possible under the current zoning, for tighter zoning seemed in the wind.

The Jefferson County Planning Commission was horrified. The plat chopped up the tract into 1,875 lots —and at the expense of most of the natural features. "Ruthless treatment of a beautiful countryside" said the planning commission's staff.

During this time the success of the Colonial Park town house development in Louisville was prompting developers to think more about cluster. The owner of the Hunting Creek property retained the landscape architects who had done the site plan for Colonial Park— Miller, Wihry and Brooks.

The result is a fine demonstration of how cluster can capitalize on the natural features that conventional plans most often destroy. The plan is outstanding in its provision of recreational areas. There is a golf course, riding club, sledding hill, boat club and a network of woodland trails. These features, moreover, are skillfully woven throughout the tract and many do double duty as buffers between developments. The plan is also outstanding in its mixture of housing types and its provision for community facilities.

While the first houses won't be ready until spring, the builders have been doing some advertising to get the feel of the market. The interest in the town houses is proving much stronger than expected and the proportion will probably be increased.

Westchester

In this 366 acre development on the outskirts of Springfield, Illinois, Planner Richard Selleg has made the Radburn type superblock the heart of the project and has threaded a pedestrian walkway and park system through the middle of it. Several of the smaller blocks on the periphery have been treated in the same fashion.

In the first superblock to be built, in the northeast corner of the site, the central green demonstrates how well aesthetics and economics can complement each other. A swale of about 25 acres ran through the center of this portion; by landscaping it into a common green the developer saved himself some $10,000 worth of storm drainage pipe.

The sponsors of Westchester sell lots to individuals and to small developers; they believe this will lead to the variety hard to achieve in large projects. The bulk of the 1,143 units planned will be single family houses, but the plan has set aside space for town houses.

Ville du Parc

Back in 1959 the Milwaukee suburb of Mequon retained planner William Nelson to draw up a general plan for the community. Nelson's imaginative plan emphasized

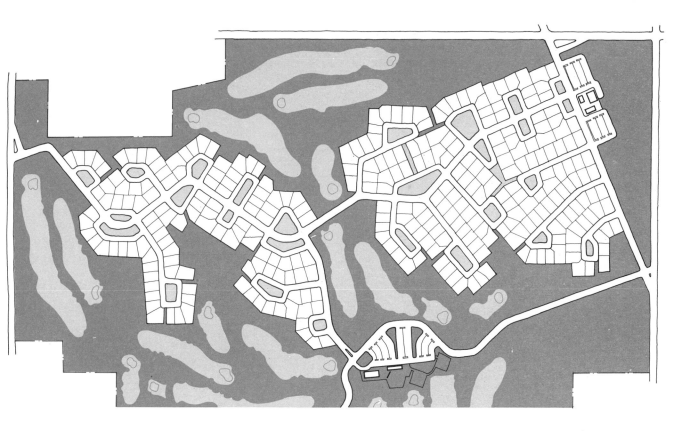

Ville du Parc plan groups houses around courts.

open space conservation through land acquisition, easements and flood plain zoning. But this alone wouldn't be enough. Nelson urged that the town also encourage cluster development, and he sketched a hypothetical example to show how well it could work. The town liked the idea, and approved a cluster ordinance.

A developer who had been planning a golf course subdivision also liked the idea and asked Nelson to draw up a cluster plan. Ville du Parc was the result.

Nelson reduced lot sizes and grouped them around small interior courts. Because of this grouping, 440 of the total 600 acres could be left open. Most of this is taken up by the golf course, which is threaded with woods and bridle trails.

Nearby, two other projects designed by Nelson are going up: Lac du Cours, a lakeside cluster subdivision, and Georgetown East which, somewhat contrary to its title, is a non-town house development featuring detached houses in cul-de-sac clusters.

Sea Pines

This 5,200 acre resort development on Hilton Head Island, South Carolina, shows how well the cluster idea can be adapted to the development of ocean front property. The basic plan, drawn up by Sasaki-Walker Associates, groups the lots in a series of clusters between the

"Interlocking finger" plan for Sea Pines cluster.

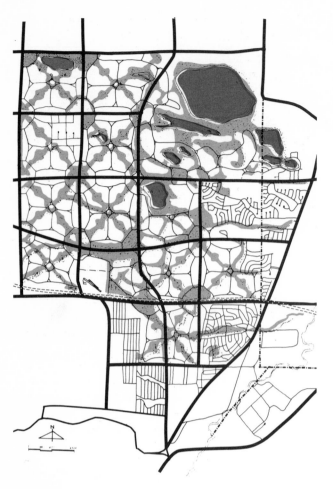

main road and the beach. The common open space is the beachfront. Fifty-foot wide walkways, owned and maintained by the developer, link all the lots with the beach. Vehicular roads lead from the interior of the cluster back to the main road. Because of the excellent circulation and pedestrian access to the beach, the rear lots are much more valuable than they would otherwise be. (Front lots, approximately 90 x 200 feet, sell for around $10,000; back lots, about 50% smaller, for about $4,000.)

The same walkway and cluster system has been used for lots around a 125 acre golf course and along a series of lagoons and canals. A feature of the master plan is the setting aside of 1,660 acres as a permanent woodland. A guarantee of this tract is written in the sales contract. Only about 1/5 of this could have been developed in any event and over the long run it should considerably enhance the value of the developed land.

Columbine Community

Ordinarily, a comprehensive community design for the development of a large area is almost impossible unless the tract is under one ownership. The plan for the 7,000 acre Columbine Community just southwest of Denver is an interesting exception. Here, twelve landowners decided to join together and have a master plan drawn up that would unify the separate developments they were contemplating.

For the planners that they retained—Harman, O'Donnell and Henninger Associates of Denver—it was to be a

Columbine Community master plan.

Plan for Lakehurst section of Columbine Community.

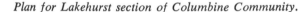

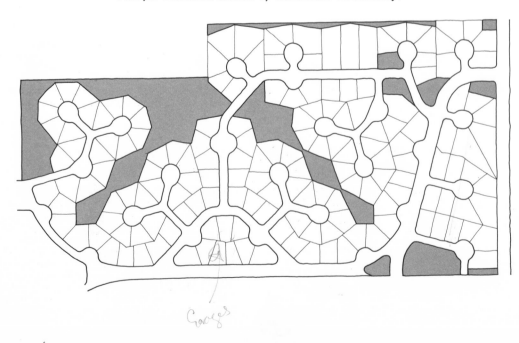

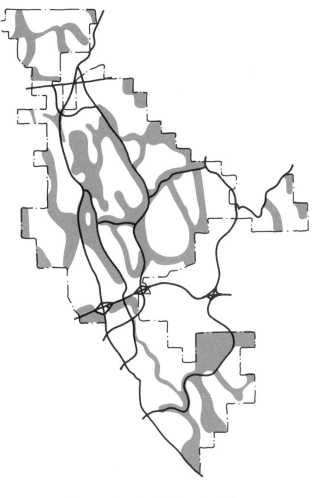

Master plan for El Dorado Hills.

textbook example. This is the firm that prepared the Urban Land Institute's influential study on new approaches to residential land development. When they went to work on the follow up study several years later, the Columbine plan could be one of the principle examples ("Innovations vs. Traditions in Community Development." Technical Bulletin 47, $6; Urban Land Institute, 1200 18th Street, Washington, D.C.)

The plan knits the separate subdivisions together with an unusually well defined circulation and open space system. The first unit to be built—the Lakehurst subdivision—reproduces the pattern of the overall community. The key unit is the cul-de-sac, with detached houses on pie-shaped lots. Half of the houses are faced towards the park area. Sidewalks encircle each cluster and are so linked that children have safe access to school and recreation areas. The proportion of common open space—about 14%—is not large, but in this semiarid area park land costs as much to install as roads and the need for continuous irrigation can lead to fairly sizeable development and maintenance expenses.

El Dorado Hills

For one of the most audacious new town efforts a group of large investors bought up some 9,800 acres of foothill land 23 miles east of Sacramento. It is a beautiful piece of land with the rolling, oak dotted hills so characteristic of California, and ideal for the large scale application of the cluster principle. Victor Gruen Associates drew up a master plan which clusters the development into a series of twelve villages with the bulk of the land remaining open.

El Dorado Hills is to be an all-year community—the primary market is the defense plant complex 10 miles to the west—but it makes recreation and the good life a major motif of the plan. As in Reston and New Seabury, each village is to be centered around a particular recreational activity. There will be golf courses—one is already up—riding trails, swimming clubs, and a marina at the south end of Lake Folsom, a state owned recreation reservoir.

The first village, much of which had been platted before the master plan was done, is a fairly conventional layout of detached houses. There is a swimming club, shopping center, and at the entrance on heavily travelled Route 50, a large public golf course. (Eventually part of this golf course area will become a regional shopping center.)

The basic houses range from $22,000 to $26,000. Unlike most California subdivisions, there will be no forest of TV antennas or utility wires. Wiring is underground and antennas are built into the attic space of the houses.

For the second unit, Governor's Village, the planners started with a clean slate. They have massed the open space so that the large surrounding spaces are linked to the center of the project and here they have grouped the school, church and recreational center sites. As in the other villages, some of the open space is to be deeded to the county as parkland, with most of the neighborhood space deeded to a community services district—in effect, a homeowners' association.

How well El Dorado Hills will do in the market place will take some time to gauge, but in one respect it is clearly superlative. For promotional razzle-dazzle there is nothing to match it. There has been a heavy schedule of radio and TV, a succession of special events, some extraordinary literature, featuring, among other things, a brochure of art photographs with captions by Walt Whitman, a letter from Governor Brown saluting the development, and an assortment of brochures and leaflets

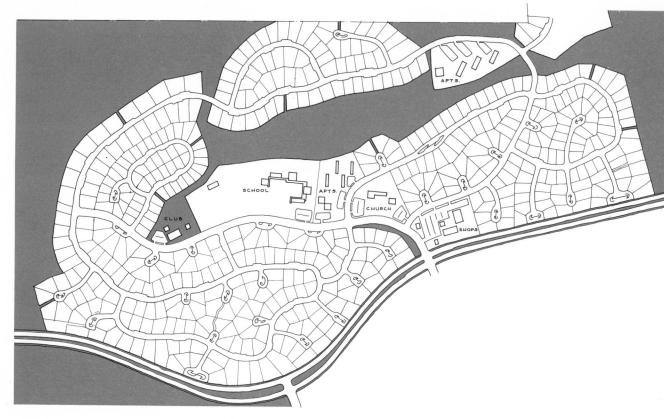

Plan of Governor's Village, El Dorado Hills.

and article reprints that could fill the trunk of a car. In a particularly successful tie-in, *Sunset Magazine* used Governor's Village as the site of its 1963 Discovery House of New Ideas—a handsome apotheosis of the California way of life that proved a great traffic builder.

Greenhaven '70

This plan which won the NAHB's 1963 award for the finest job of community planning, envisages a wide range of housing types and community facilities for a 708 acre tract in a loop of the Sacramento River in the undeveloped southern portion of the city.

The bulk of the acreage will be given over to single family homes—1,600 units in all. Later phases of the project call for a large shopping center at one end of the project and at the Sacramento River end, apartment house clusters and an elaborate marina and "boatel."

The layout of the lots, most in parallel loop streets, is standard. The outstanding feature of the plan is the way site planner David Whittett has arranged the open spaces to provide interior linkage. The open space network runs through the middle of the tract, and through the provision of overpasses and underpasses, will make

it possible for residents to reach the key park, school and shopping areas without ever having to cross a street.

While there is to be a mixture of housing types, as in virtually all of the "new towns" the mixture starts at a

Pedestrian underpass at Greenhaven '70.

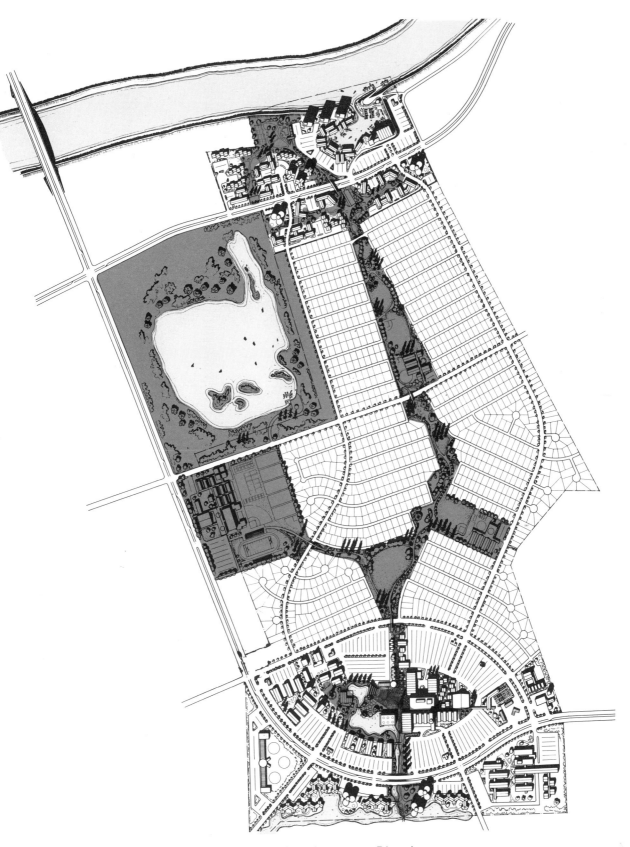

Greenhaven '70 plan: Sacramento River is at top.

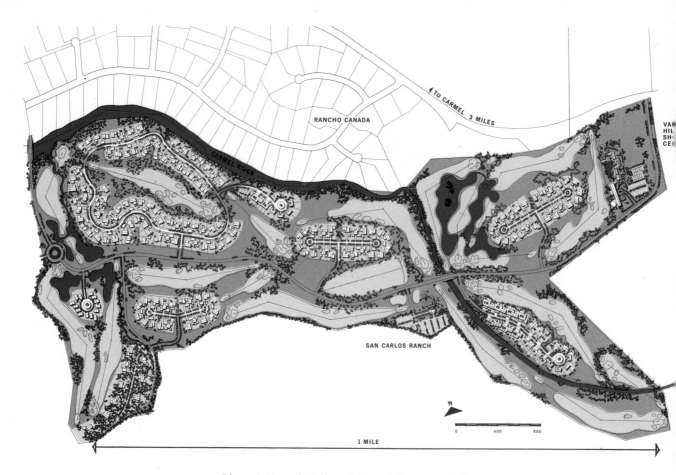

Plan of Carmel Valley Golf and Country Club.

fairly high price. Greenhaven's developers sell lots to individual builders, and houses so far constructed are custom or semi-custom, ranging from $22,000 to $50,000.

The entire "pocket" area along this part of the Sacramento River has been incorporated into a general development plan drawn up by the Sacramento Planning Commission. It consists of a total of 4,674 acres held by a number of separate owners, and to insure that the developments will be tied together with a good street and open space network, the Planning Commission—somewhat like Philadelphia's did for the Far Northeast—has done a good bit of the developers' future land planning for them. Unfortunately, while there will be many neighborhood open spaces, the general plan does not borrow the linkage idea used both by Philadelphia and by Greenhaven '70 itself, and most of the separate spaces will not tie in one with the other.

Whittett has subsequently done a community development plan for a 520 acre development in Milpitas, California. It is similar in providing a continuous park system weaving throughout the tract. It is also similar in being

something of a rescue job. Whittett was brought in after it became apparent that earlier, conventional plans were found wanting.

Carmel Valley Golf and Country Club

For some years the most celebrated cluster design was that of planners Hall and Goodhue for High Meadow, to be built in Carmel, California. Somewhat to the embarrassment of cluster advocates, it has yet to be built. But it set a lot of developers thinking, and among the results are the striking plans done by Hall and Goodhue for the two developments illustrated here. They show a similar feel for the land, and they *are* being built.

One of the layouts, set on the floor of the Carmel Valley, is a deft example of a golf course cluster subdivision. The Carmel River is the dominant element; its tree lined banks meander through the site, and to go nature one better it has been tapped to create several small lakes. Unlike many golf course subdivisions, the houses do not ring the course; most are set in cluster groups within the course. There will be 168 detached houses, on 10 to 12,000 square foot lots, and 42 town

Plan of Skyline Forest saves woods: note contrast with conventional plats nearby.

house apartment units. The common land, 153 of the total 245 acres, will be maintained by the club.

Skyline Forest

More unusual is the development plan for a steep, forested slope overlooking Monterey. This happens to be a key feature of the city's landscape, and as consultants to the planning commission, Hall and Goodhue had previously urged that the forest ridge be conserved as a greenbelt; where development did take place, the ridge would not be notched and scarred nor the view from the city below ruined.

Local developer Wright Fisher agreed with these objectives, and when he acquired the tract from an out of town developer he asked Hall and Goodhue to draw up a site plan for it.

Their plan keeps the visual continuity of the wooded skyline. The houses will be clustered in such a way that half the tract will be left in its natural state, including 89 acres as a forest preserve. Property owners will hold an undivided interest in the open space. As in many other California cluster developments, a special service district coincident with the subdivision will be set up for the maintenance of the open space.

There will be quite a mixture of housing types. Single family homes, 210 in all, will be set close together in clusters of six to eight apiece. Where the ridge is steepest, there will be clusters of town houses and apartment units, with decks and retaining walls, Sausalito fashion. In the very thickest part of the forest will be something of a cross-up: town houses set around a formal urban square. Nearby will be a club for the whole area, with swimming pool and tennis courts.

There will be no gas street lamps.

Chapter IX

LINKAGE

IN the last two chapters we have been dealing with cluster developments one by one. This is how most communities have been dealing with them too — as they come up, one by one. This is understandable, but unless a further step is taken soon the result will be more sprawl, only a little bit better. There could be small attractive subdivisions, to quote *California Tomorrow*, "and a hopeless slurb of small attractive subdivisions."

Cannot the separate spaces be linked together? Here is the great opportunity for cluster. The open space of a cluster subdivision may be functional in itself, but it becomes far more so if it is tied in with other open spaces —with community parks, with schools, and with the open spaces of other cluster developments. The total acreage is not the significant figure: it would be little more than the sum of the spaces that would be provided in any event. What can make the acres so effective is the fact of linkage, and a few relatively small pieces can often make the critical difference.

It may be years before all the pieces are fitted but the opportunity for communities to get going is immediate. Developers are amenable; for self-interest many are going to plan common open spaces anyway, and it is no more trouble for them to put the spaces so they mesh with the community open space plan than not. But they have to be asked.

This means that the community has to have a pretty good idea of the framework it wants. It does not, fortunately, require an interminable effort at a full master plan. Nature has already done a good bit of work along these lines and the drainage network that it has cut into the area can furnish the spine of an excellent plan. A stream is the most obvious example: if it is a beautiful stretch so much the better, but a humdrum watercourse —even one that is dry most of the time—can have a great unifying effect.

Let's look at a few pilot efforts. One is furnished by Santa Barbara County, California. Several years ago the County adopted an open space ordinance to encourage developers to provide open space in exchange for reduction of lot sizes. Developers were glad to take advantage of it, for the area where the new subdivisions are going up is crossed by a series of dry creek ravines that are useless for building. The spaces, averaging out to about 12% of the area, are in most cases dedicated to a homeowners association; the county retains a conservation easement on the spaces and for maintenance they are annexed to a county service district with the power to levy assessments.

At first the result promised to be a hodge-podge of scattered spaces. But there is an underlying order. The ravines, coming down from the mountains to the sea, are a natural framework by which the separate open spaces can be connected, and the county's master plan calls for strategically located regional parks and community play areas to help tie the whole thing together. The ravines don't look like much now; one day they may be priceless.

Santa Clara County to the north furnishes another example. Its flat valley floor has been ravaged by a scatteration of subdivisions, but running down from the coastal mountains to San Francisco Bay are several dry creek courses still relatively unspoiled. Planning director Karl Belser has seen in them the best means for an open space chain that will provide recreation and at the same time give definition to the area.

Most of these creek areas fall under different kinds of ownership—golf courses, county parks, state highway rights of way, utilities, and town parks. The crux of the problem is to tie all these compatible spaces together by filling in the missing links, and in most cases this need not involve a great deal of additional acreage. The Stevens Creek chain shown at right, for example, would add up to 1,700 acres—and only 509 acres remain to be acquired.

Some of these portions could be provided by developers through cluster planning. Equally important, the main corridor could be complemented by a sort of tributary system along the smaller creek courses that feed

Santa Clara County plan makes creek chain unifying element for built-up area.

into it, with bridle trails and paths tying them together. This network would be ideal for high density cluster developments and for eventual redevelopment of old subdivisions.

Santa Clara County has also been pioneering the idea of utility rights of way as a connective link. Along much the same axis as the creeks, the valley floor is criss-crossed by a utility network for high tension lines and for waterways, running between 60 to 100 feet wide and in aggregate amounting to about 1,000 acres. Usually, such areas are regarded as an eyesore, and they are left to weeds and rubbish. Under Santa Clara's "Greenway" proposal they are to be landscaped into an 8 mile network with "nodules" of open space provided by 18 school sites. The utilities like the idea and while there is a good bit of negotiating still to be done some portions have already been developed for recreation use and the water conservation district has started landscaping some of its canals.

THE highway can be another unifying element. Aesthetically it is usually the opposite as far as subdivisions are concerned, but this need not be; another California county, Monterey, is demonstrating that if highway planning and cluster planning are integrated the two can complement each other very nicely.

Monterey County has always been very zealous in protecting its magnificent scenery. It was not only the first county in the United States to zone against billboards in rural areas, but more recently has taken the lead in getting the state to launch a scenic highway program. As presently envisioned, this program calls for a cooperative effort of the counties and the state to preserve the scenic corridor for certain highways to be designated.

Monterey County is not waiting. It has a quite clear idea of the corridors it wants to protect and is taking steps to designate them as "scenic conservation districts." In these districts the county is going to control access and will establish special architectural, site and landscape controls for any building that will take place. It will establish residential densities. Developers will be encouraged to put their utilities underground and will be given special inducements to plan their open spaces so that they will contribute to the scenic view from the highway as well as provide recreation and amenity for the residents.

The first scenic corridor is along famous Highway 1 on the coast; indeed, one of the things that promoted the county's push for scenic highways was the suspicion that the state highway department would love to cut and fill this beautiful sweep of coast into a giant freeway. The county has designated the visual area and has already gained some contributions. One developer, for example, has been induced to concentrate his development on the portion upland of the road and to dedicate either a scenic easement or the fee to the strip bordering the ocean. Another will provide a conservation easement on a portion of the highway and dedicate roughly 7 acres as a greenbelt. A group of land owners has dedicated an easement on 12½ acres of the heavily wooded slopes which form a background to the Bixby Canyon Bridge, one of the outstanding attractions of the coast.

Another key highway traverses the rolling grassland between Monterey and Salinas. Fortunately, large-scale development is just starting and the first few subdivisions are good precedents. In the site planning, explains county planning director Edward DeMars, "we are

79

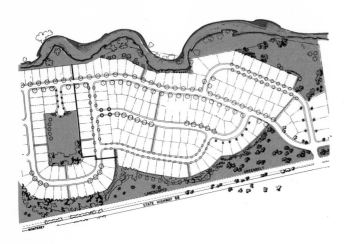

Subdivision open space furnishes scenic border for highway.

trying to integrate the open space planning of the development so that it provides a scalloped effect along the highway. We are emphasizing two things: one, that the planting must be native to the area; second, that the plantings must be pulled back to provide a sense of openness rather than a landscaped tunnel."

The subdivision pictured above, Toro Park, is a case in point. Note that the open space was planned so that it does double duty; it will furnish an excellent recreation area for the residents and at the same time buffer and enhance the highway. This particular subdivision is in flat land and one of the problems was how to assure that the open space would be landscaped, for there is little or no natural vegetation. The county's solution was to require the subdivider to improve the open space and to back this up by a performance bond, as with other improvements.

The case of the Laguna Seca Ranch Estates provides a somewhat opposite problem; it is rolling land, dotted with oaks. Through careful site planning only two trees will have been removed. The developer deeded 2.5 acres to the country along the highway and a scenic easement on the 4.5 acres of open space to be used by the residents.

"It is well to re-emphasize," says DeMars, "that for this program to be entirely successful it is necessary to establish densities for given areas, thereby determining the improvement need and a basis on which to discuss alternate means of development . . . If a developer can be shown where he can save money through an alternate method, he is more than likely for it."

When a cluster development is to be part of an open space chain the question comes up of how much of the open space should be dedicated for public use. There is no easy generalization on this. As this report argued earlier, dedication to the public should not be a flat requirement, for the interests of the homeowners in the enjoyment of common areas and public access can often be in conflict. This is a matter that has to be judged on a case-by-case basis.

The experience to date suggests that it poses no great difficulties. In the same development the two kinds of ownership can complement each other. The bulk of the open space, particularly the interior commons, could work best if owned and maintained by a homeowners association with the public interest served by a conservation easement guaranteeing the openness. The part of the open space that has a connective quality, however, such as a strip along a stream, could be dedicated to the municipality: it would help fill out the public open space network and would benefit the residents of the development by linking their commons with nearby parks and schools.

I N the case we have been discussing, the public agency lays down rough guide lines and then negotiates the open space as each development comes up. Another and more far-reaching approach is for the public to lay down not only the guide lines but basic layout of the developments themselves. Philadelphia, in its plan for the Far Northeast, did just this; it laid down a street pattern that enforced cluster development and specified the precise areas that developers would have to dedicate as open space if they wanted to be able to build. Had the city asked only that a given percentage of a tract be dedicated, it might well have gotten more open space; the land, however, could have been bits and pieces rather than the continuous stream network that has been achieved.

Most communities would regard this kind of planning as too highhanded. But it worked. The developers were not troubled by ideological considerations for the plan offered them considerable advantages, not the least of them being the amount of site planning that had been done for them free by the city. Furthermore, the stream site and wooded land they had to dedicate extracted no sacrifice; they would have had to spend a lot of money grading this land, and the cluster layout allowed them to build all their houses where it was easiest to build them.

Many planners feel that eventually the public will have to take an even stronger lead. Some developers have the resources to tackle the planning of entire comnunities themselves, but there are few of them. Even in these cases, furthermore, something is wanting; excellent as these "balanced communities" may be, as far as people are concerned the balance usually starts well up on the income scale. The kind of industry that is sought is the same—well heeled, clean and light.

But whatever the shortcomings of the new towns, most planners see them as a big step in the right direction. The alternative would appear to be a host of subdivisions with little overall cohesiveness and equally short of housing for lower income groups. The mess could later be cleaned up by a suburban redevelopment program but a better bet might be to avoid it by using something like the redevelopment process to begin with. A regional authority could buy the land, make a master plan for it and then resell portions to developers who will follow it. Another approach, proposed in the new federal housing bill, would encourage developers to put up large and truly balanced communities by providing low cost loans for the land assembly.

WHETHER or not these come to pass, recent open space legislation has given communities very considerable powers for shaping development and much more can be done with the tools already at hand than most communities realize. As a minimum step, they can use the police power to zone their wetlands, flood plains, and water courses against development. The practical question is how far they can push the boundaries of the open space corridor from the center of the stream and get away with it, for there comes a point when use of the police power amounts to condemnation without compensation. Most communities, however, have been far too timid to get anywhere near the point. Conversely, the few who have done a good job have taken a rather broad view of the public interest; they have pushed the line out to include as much of their flood plains as possible — and if it's too much, let the courts tell them so later.

But zoning is only a partial step; to really anchor an open space network, acquisition is vital. This would be true whatever kind of development was contemplated; the new reality of cluster, however, can give communities a very powerful assist in negotiating with landowners.

To illustrate, let us take an area on the outer rim of suburbia, the last best chance. The key feature is a stream valley running between two towns. The flood plain, roughly several hundred yards on either side of the stream, has been zoned against development. Most of the open land, however, is quite suitable for building. Typically, it will consist of a mixture of farms, large

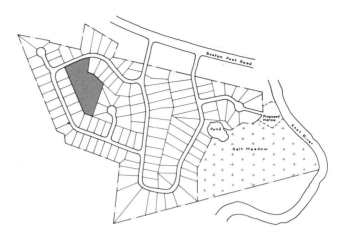

Guilford, Conn. project uses wetlands for commons.

estates, and a scattering of small holdings, and a heavy proportion of the landowners will be elderly.

There has always been a considerable gift potential in such areas, but economics has not had too much to do with it. Where gifts have been secured, the donor has most often been motivated by a general feeling for the landscape, coupled often with a strong suspicion that the heirs would waste no time in chopping it up for development. It will have been pointed out, of course, that preservation of a few key pieces will enhance the value of the remainder. This economic argument, however, as with the tax saving, has been useful chiefly as a supporting rationalization for people who are in the happy position of not having to worry about the economics.

People who do have to worry have been much more skeptical. They have been under the strong impression that developers would want to use all of the property and the idea that preservation of part of it would be good business seems much too theoretical. Farmers in particular can be quite unmoved; when they look at the meadow and that frontage along the county road, they think of the nice building lots that can be sold off. They too may feel for the land but they are more concerned with the nest egg money it promises.

The cluster concept changes this balance of self-interest. The community now has solid ground to document the case that the preservation of selected positions will, in fact as well as theory, not mean a sacrifice of market value and may, most likely, enhance it. The new conservation commissions in Massachusetts and Connecticut, which have been becoming quite proficient in the art of wheedling land, have lately begun to exploit this argument. Many are finding that it has considerable leverage power.

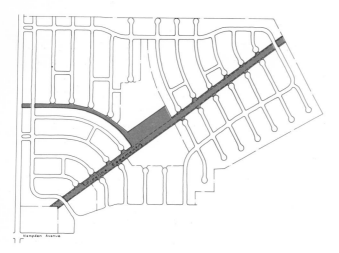

Hampden Heights subdivision in Denver makes pipeline easement main axis of greenway system.

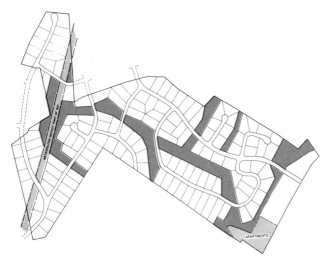

Water district right of way is part of open space plan for The Woodlands, Farmington, Conn.

In the not so hypothetical outer suburbia we have cited, the community leaders would be just as happy if development went somewhere else. In this case, however, they have decided to meet the future half-way. Hypothesizing an eventual series of developments along cluster lines they have decided to lay down the open space network while there is time. They want to get gifts and they also want to get as moderate a price as possible where purchase is necessary. In both cases their argument will go something like this:

Your 85 acres, they say to the landowner, is one of the key scenic spots in this valley. We know it is prime development land and we are not going to ask you to give up any capital gain you might wish to realize from

it. Our idea is to save the key pieces so that we may get the kind of development that is right for this area.

The community representatives unfold a map of the valley. They indicate the strip down the middle of the valley they want to acquire as a streamside park. About nine acres of the landowners' property falls in this area. They then show the secondary network of draws and creeks they'd like to see kept open; in this case about 10 acres. Could they work at something together? Perhaps he would sell them the fee to the nine acres along the stream and give an open space easement along the banks of the creeks.

This is good for the town, the negotiators continue, and we believe it is good for you. Keeping these portions open won't detract from the market price of your property. In fact, we think we can demonstrate to you that this plan will help make your property worth a good bit more. With diagrams they show that were he to develop the tract himself, he'd get more money out of his land with a design that left the draws and the creek land open. So would a developer.

The persuasiveness of this argument depends squarely on a very thorough exposition of the cluster principle, and it usually can't be done at one sitting. It has to be demonstrated to landowners that: (1) a good cluster design would call for the conservation of the areas in question; (2) that the cluster principle is not some far-off possibility but an approach that developers themselves want to use.

It is equally important to emphasize that there is an overall plan that affects other landowners as well, and that eminent domain can back it up. Contrary to a widely held assumption, this can reassure landowners. They don't want to be the patsy. If the community really means business in laying down the open space network this is to the self-interest of the landowner; for it means that his flanks will be buffered against incompatible development and the existence of the stream valley park will further enhance his property.

CAN the same principle be applied in the built-up areas nearer the city? The scale is different, the open space more constricted, and the market prices are greater. For this reason many people conclude that acquiring the fee to open space would be hideously expensive and the cost of easements almost as great. One planning study of a metropolitan area, for example, indicates the feasibility of easement purchase by coloring different sections according to the average market price of the land. Close in, where the verage is $10,000 and up per acre, the chart says no ɔ. The reasoning is that the bulk of the price is based n development value; ergo, to acquire the open space asements would cost almost as much as the fee.

But let us take a closer look at the land. The average ɡure can be highly misleading. A developer who pays 400,000 for 100 acres is not paying $4,000 for each cre. The market value is apt to be concentrated in a ortion which, if he had to buy separately, he would ay $15,000 or $20,000 an acre for. As assessors well ecognize, there can be wide variations within a tract nd on their map some of the acres in woodland, or in teep ravines, or marshland, may be valued at only a raction of the other.

These sections are the hardest to develop; by the same ɔken, they are likely to be just the kind of land most uitable for the community's open space. Whether the ommunity is dealing with the developer or with a land-ɔwner who is contemplating eventual sale for develop-ɲent, there is a good bargain to be struck.

Easements are particularly useful in such situations. n soliciting open space well in advance of development t should be remembered that though the eventual de-ɛeloper may not wish to build on the marginal land ɪe will want to have title to most of it, if only for a while. ʰe gross acreage helps determine the number of units ɪe can get up and though he may deed the open space ɔ the community or to the homeowners, he wants to have redit for it before he does.

I ɴ discussing linkage we have been emphasizing the importance of small open spaces. It is admit-tedly a dangerous point for it can easily be mis- used by those who would be only too happy to have ɔpen spaces small and not much else. Before going any urther, therefore, let us reiterate that if we have to err n any direction let it by all means be towards more ɔpen space.

But a good cause does not exempt us from competitive ɔressures. The dominant trend is towards more inten-ɪive land use, and this applies to the use of open space ust as much as it does to building space. High land ɔrices may be a disadvantage, but they are also a dis-ɔipline, and just as they have forced developers to press ɔr more concentration, so should they force planners ɔ get much more out of each acre of open space.

The conventional greenbelt concept needs a thorough ɛexamination. In laying down general plans for metro-ɔolitan areas it has become almost reflex to color the ɲap with great swaths of green space, often many miles wide. Their importance in such plans is not what they will provide, but what they will prevent; their primary function is to squeeze development into a more orderly pattern. Other open space benefits are duly noted — light, airy, breathing space, etc. — but the plans are generally rather hazy on this score, with terms such as "land reserve," "natural resource areas" and the like indicating that the technical matter of how they are to be kept open will be thrashed out sometime in the future.

Let us assume for the moment that it would. How functional would such green belts be? For separation, and enhancing new development their usefulness is con-centrated along the edges. But this is only a fraction of the total; as far as the residents are concerned a 300 foot wide strip of woodland would give much the same effect. In the new communities such plans call for, furthermore, the bulk of the residents won't live near the edges: they will be concentrated in the high density tower and the town house areas in the center. Out towards the periphery the densities diminish, with the result that the greenbelt is closest to the people on the larger lots who need it the least.

Let us turn to the interior of the greenbelts. Here the question of function is critical. Recreation areas would fill part, but what about the rest of the umpteen square miles? It is hard enough to save open space where the overlay of benefits is compelling — where, for example, a flood plain does double duty as a recrea-tion area. It is harder yet when the land is quite buildable, and near the city to boot.

The English experience is instructive. Even with tight planning controls, greenbelts drawn with a wide brush have proved difficult to defend against encroachment. Where a greenbelt has been tailored more tightly, how-ever it has stood up to pressure quite well.

Most of our proposed greenbelts are farm land. Un-questionably, it would be nice if all such land were to remain open, and generalized statements about breathing room, encouragement of agriculture, and so on can easily be invoked in support. But this is not enough. To save anything the plan has to get down to cases. If farmland is highly productive so much the better, but there has to be a strong and quite specific case that a particular open space packs in a maximum of other benefits. And if the public wishes these benefits it must be ready to back up its case with money.

It will be paper open space otherwise. By happen-stance the writer had to make a study on open space tax assessment in an area part of which had been designated as a metropolitan open space reserve. It seemed to be farm land. A check of county courthouse records, however, revealed that farmers didn't own the land. They had sold out long since to a syndicate at $2,000 an acre and up. To take advantage of the assessment law, the syndicate had let the farmers stay on the land so it would be taxed on the low agricultural basis until the time for building was at hand. On the map this is colored soothing green.

We do not have to resign ourselves to speculative pressures. We should be prepared to buy land where necessary, and if the price is high, so is its usefulness. But we had better well heed the lesson of the market-place. The greenbelt vision gives a falsely reassuring picture of what is achieveable and thus obscures from us the overriding necessity of sewing up the land that counts most and doing it now.

Linkage, not gross acreage, is the key. With all the ingenuity we can muster we must try and fit together a host of elements — an experimental farm, a private golf course, the right of way of a new freeway, a local park, a community nature center, the spaces of cluster subdivisions, research parks, pipeline easements, stream-side parks. The result will not be the "natural land-scape," but it could not be. The landscape has always been man made, and it must inevitably reflect changes of use. This does not mean our open spaces must be artificial; where they seem too manicured, too self-conscious, or primly green this is not art but a lack of it.

We could take a cue from Capability Brown and the eighteenth century landscape architects. That epitome of the "natural" landscape, the English countryside, is to a considerable degree an invention. The clump of trees on a distant hill, the simple mill pond — these were often carefully planned and their execution in-volved a prodigious amount of work, sometimes including the levelling of hills or the building of abandoned villages. There was artifice, to be sure, but it did not proclaim itself; Brown always kept uppermost in his mind's eye the eye of the beholder.

There is infinitely more reason to do so today. Our spaces are fewer, our patrons more difficult. They are people who will live in these areas, who will drive its roads, use its schools: our network must be conceived from their point of view, quite literally, rather than the birds-eye perspective of the map or the scale model.

It is the *feeling* of space we must provide. This is not the same as space; our subjective reactions are as important, and as the reader can test for himself, a few key pieces often dominate our perception of a much larger area. The Taconic Parkway, running north from New York, is a good case in point. A great many people believe it is by far the most pleasant super highway in the East, and if you asked them why, they would tell you that it is because most of it runs through open farmland. It doesn't. Check its 90 odd miles and you will find that there are only a few stretches that are bordered by farms. A far greater proportion is in the densely wooded area that many people find somewhat boring. This is the reality. What people *see,* however, is a reality too, and the more important one.

With art, then, we can link the parts of our urban landscape into a very effective whole. In gross acreage, such networks may be smaller than the large greenbelt; in effectiveness they can be far greater. They can be woven throughout the urban area, where people will see them and use them, as part of their daily life — not a relief from the environment; but *within* it.

Chapter X

THE HANDLING OF SPACE

THE smaller spaces within developments present the same alternative. Should the open spaces serve design primarily, or should they be for people? In large projects, especially redevelopment projects, the spirit underlying the Greenbelt approach has generally been the rule. They favor abstract space; characteristically, urban redevelopment projects consist of a group of towers set symmetrically in vast malls of green. In the bird's-eye perspective from which they were designed, the space is functional. It is for the architect. It sets off his towers, gives order, unity, visual coherence to his design.

The space is not for people. These expanses are to be gazed at, not used, and lest anyone miss the point, the grass is carefully chained from human trespass. Peremptory signs saying don't do this and don't do that are everywhere. Children, especially, are regarded as a menace.

The momentum of this approach seems destined to carry on for some time longer. New York is so far gone in this direction as to seem beyond redemption; newspapers could use the same illustration over and over again for almost every new housing project, low rent or high, and the illustration could date back to the '30's, for all the difference anyone could note. Why a city with such great resources of design talent should be so reactionary is a puzzle, but with few exceptions the new projects continue to be the most hackneyed and brutal in the country.

Elsewhere, fortunately, a decided reaction against the barracks approach has set in. For years critics argued that a mixture of housing types would be far more pleasant, and a few early projects which combined towers with duplex houses and courts demonstrated that it was quite economic, as well as more pleasing. Invariably, the market demand was strongest for the duplex units. It took an interminable time for the machinery of redevelopment to incorporate the lessons but now, at last, in a number of cities some really good projects are going through.

The best make much more efficient use of space. In some cases the ground coverage and density is higher than in the conventional high rise projects, but the effect of space is actually greater. For one thing, the larger common spaces have been made much more pleasant by being given a sense of enclosure. Instead of using open space as a setting for the buildings, with the space dribbling out to surrounding streets, the spaces are given a more intimate character by enclosing them within the building groups.

But the most significant shift is towards the private open space. In the heirarchy of spaces, it has long been evident that the small, intimate space is the most precious of all to people. The success of Baldwin Hills should have proved this emphatically; its patios and smaller open spaces have proved admirably functional, while the three large common greens have been used less than was originally expected. The predilection of project designers for abstract spaces, however, led them to draw the wrong lesson. The larger spaces seem to give visual coherence; the smaller to make the design "busy." Rather than provide both kinds, the designers concentrated on the common space.

The new projects which combine both kinds of spaces do tend to be a bit messy in comparison to the conventional project, but this defect, if such it is, is troublesome only when you are looking down at models. In actuality, the smaller private open spaces tend to enliven the scene for the people in the towers. Even when low buildings and patios fill up space that otherwise would have been left empty, the total effect can be more pleasing.

CLUSTER developments outside the city would seem to mark an opposite trend; larger common areas, smaller private. But the shift is more statistical than anything else. In suburban cluster developments, as well as in urban projects, the private spaces are the most important to people and in general they seem to have been handled very well.

The trickiest problem is the relationship between the private and the common spaces. In most town house developments there is a very definite separation, with high fences or walls enclosing the patio. This gives maximum privacy but it reduces the ability of the two kinds of areas to borrow space from each other. In some projects, by contrast, the private spaces merge with the common, with no demarcation or only a very low hedge or wall, thus providing more expanse but less privacy. There is no one solution, certainly, but experience suggests that for most people privacy is the more important consideration, and clear separation eliminates the ambiguities that can be so troublesome when people live close together.

There is enough room for both kinds of space The private space requires only a small fraction of the total acreage. Patio dimensions, a check of the tabulation in the appendix will reveal, are fairly consistent; the width of the house largely determines them and 20 by 20 feet seems to be the median.

The variable is the commons. It can be too large, though this danger is rather theoretical. Developers are finding that with good design it is remarkable how much feeling of space can be given by even a small commons. Undoubtedly, some developers would like to experiment along these lines even further, but the community has the means to discipline this urge. Densities would have to get much higher than they are now before there would be any real dilemma in the provision of both kinds of space.

The message, as conveyed by typical New York redevelopment projects, is NO. But the open space costs enough. Why not have people use it? To restrict such high cost land to only one use is atrocious economics.

Standardization, not compression, seems to be the real danger. Even at this early date a rather well defined basic module has become apparent, and as the reader has undoubtedly noted in going over the site plans, this is particularly the case with town house projects. Their combinations of patios and small commons are very similar and some are virtually identical.

The basic design is a good one. But that is part of the trouble; it is so serviceable — and marketable — that there is a very strong likelihood that many devel-

opers will copy it intact, whatever the topography of the site or surrounding neighborhood, and won't bother to try fresh approaches.

THERE are many to explore. Do the commons, for example, have to be green? Grass and greenery may be salubrious, but there can be too much of it, and some of the most celebrated garden city communities suffer from the over-emphasis. Without enclosure, or a striking foreground or background, expanses of green can be quite dull, and sometimes they can be downright oppressive.

Punctuation and contrast are needed, and one of the best ways to provide them is through the paved courtyard or small plaza. It can provide an excellent common area, and tends to heighten the effect of the green there is. In few settings does a large tree seem so effective. The paved court also makes a nice transition between the private open space and the surrounding common areas, all the more so if the housing clusters are surrounded by large expanses of green.

The paved court, however, still strikes many people as much too revolutionary for the market. One of the most promising developments in the country, for example, is now stalled over this question. The site planner had set his clusters in the middle of a golf course. Since there was to be such an expanse of green surrounding them, he planned the common space within each cluster as a paved courtyard. The developer asked a market consultant to give his judgment. Too far out, the consultant advised. Reasoning backwards on the basis of what had sold before, he recommended that the spaces be grass and look "pretty and soft."

Such timidity is unwarranted, even by commercial standards. The court has been given a pretty good consumer test for quite a few centuries, and where it has been tried anew it seems to work as well as ever. Charles Goodman's paved courts for the River Park development in Washington are a fine example. Compared to architect Chlothiel Smith's grassy spaces in the neighboring Capitol Park development, Goodman's courts could seem a bit severe, but both projects have sold well and in both the open spaces seem to work quite well — proving, once again, that different approaches can achieve equally satisfying results.

CHILDREN'S play areas offer another challenge. Children seem to play almost everywhere else. The architect and developer are likely to assure you that this is not so; that the children's areas have worked out just as planned — and they see what they believe. Perhaps we visited at the wrong time, but in the majority of developments we studied, the designated play areas were under-used, and even the free form play sculpture that so intrigues the adult eye didn't seem to have much drawing power for children.

The children go where the action is, and the action most usually is on the streets and alleys and parking courts. Here's where the deliverymen deliver their goods, where fathers wash their cars on weekends, and where children have the most room for wheeling around on their own vehicles.

This mixing of traffic is exactly what many planners have sought most to avoid, but is there not a lesson here? If children repeatedly seek out such areas, planners should ride with the punch and make use of this fact of life. Safety demands some separation, but if paved courts are going to be used by the children in any event, it would make sense to plan them deliberately with that in mind.

There is need, of course, for formal play areas, particularly for very young children, and fencing is often necessary. In many cases, however, the fencing is redundant. Observe the use of these areas and you will note that the children who go are taken there by mothers; and where there is no playground director there are usually several adults.

Play areas are most deficient in providing for older children. As the National Recreation Association has pointed out, the kind of formal play space they need must be large enough for organized sports, and there must be a good bit of hard surface. Too many play areas are a sort of no-man's land—too large for small children, too small for the older.

Follow the children and there are other lessons to be learned. They like clutter, forbidden clutter best of all, and they show a marked antipathy to barriers and signs telling them what not to do. Site plans can't be too permissive about all this, obviously, or there would be no peace for the adults in the development. But the children's instincts are not wholly juvenile and a site plan which recognizes them can be quite effective.

One of the best public housing projects in the country is Easter Hill, outside San Francisco. The site was a rocky hillside, but rather than bulldoze it away, architects Vernon DeMars and Donald Hardison left the rocks pretty much as they were, and although they did provide some playground equipment, they conceived the hill site as something of a playground itself. Those who like the order of the standard public housing project find it messy, but children love it. They roam all over—there are no chains—and to the adult eye, as

Where the action is: paved garage areas at Pomeroy Green get heavy traffic from children.

a result, the place has a wonderfully amiable quality.

For many other reasons topography should be exploited much more than it has been. Aside from their attraction for children, rocks and hillocks make a much more interesting layout, and if nature doesn't provide them, the developer can. It is often more economic for him to do this than not to. It costs him money to haul the overburden away; with less expenditure he can make it into an asset. Central Park can still teach us lessons on this score. It seems like a vast expanse, but thanks to the way that Olmsted worked with the terrain, at eye level it is a series of spaces, some of them quite intimate.

Open spaces and buildings have a strong influence on each other, and it is important to have architects design houses for the cluster layout — or, at the very least, to have architects design the houses. Up to a point the conventional builder's house can marry fairly well with a cluster layout; as the density increases, however, the two work at cross purposes. The typical rancher, designed for a wide suburban lot, throws everything into the facade on the front side, thus emphasizing the opposite axis suitable for cluster layout. Worse yet, the typical facade variations, which are mercifully separated by wide lots, clash very badly when they are brought together.

But the architectural challenge is not merely the design of a good cluster house; it is to dovetail the housing and the space so that they work for each other. Few aspects of cluster are so unexploited. If we are going to have interior commons, for example, why not follow through and adapt the buildings for real enclosure? Open space is at its most inviting when it is approached through a covered passageway, yet this ancient principle has been little applied. Neither has the use of the crescent or the arcade or the circus.

Too many developers rely on gimmicks to give visual interest which the basic design lacks, and since they all use the same gimmicks — those Baltimore gas lamps, for example — the result is uniformity. Focal points that are an integral part of the architecture are far more effective. Larry Freel's design for Creekside is an exam-

Planned play area at Pomeroy Green.

Alleys at Radburn are fine, if unintended, playgrounds.

Capitol Park: spontaneity in the smaller spaces.

ple; an open stairway, admirably functional in itself, serves as a very attractive frame for a swimming pool and patio. And why aren't there more fountains?

SIZE may have something to do with this lack of imagination. In evaluating the effect of open space and building design a number of people have come independently to the same conclusion: the big projects seem less pleasing than the small ones. There are exceptions; but the big projects tend to look like projects, even in their smaller components. This is true in Europe as well as in America and it can happen even where the designers are of the first order.

One moral would be not to build large projects at all, but this is not very helpful. Whether planned and built by private developers or by public authorities, more large-scale projects are going to be put up. The practical course is to ask what the built-in defects are — and which ones we can do something about.

The ability to design a whole new community from scratch and to foresee successfully all of its intricate physical and social relationships is given to few mortals, if any, either as individuals or in collaboratives. The sheer size of a large project, however, unfortunately invites a certain arrogance. With such a large site to work with, the planner can feel impelled to arrive at an ideal plan and impose it on the site, rather than let

the topography and the neighboring environment help shape the plan. To compound the problem further, the separate units of the communities are usually designed all at once and they are often constructed more or less simultaneously.

In any plan there are bound to be some mistakes. The trouble with the large project is that it can rob planners of the chance to profit by the mistakes. A

Carl Koch's Liberty Square uses overburden for commons.

whole set of assumptions has been frozen into the design and it is very difficult for people who made the assumptions to recognize which are not working out. Even if they could, in many cases it would be too late. All the construction is done, or too far along to replan.

Some of the most successful features of residential developments have been changes arrived at through trial and error in building the first sections. The serpentine wall patios at Baldwin Hills, for example, were not in the original plan. Fenced patios were provided, and only for ground floor units. When these proved highly successful, the serpentine walls were added to create additional patios.

If there is to be a large-scale project, it would seem best to lay down a general plan but to do the detailed planning only for the first components to be built. For this reason the difficulties private developers have in getting financing sufficient to go ahead with a huge project full steam can be something of a blessing. All of the super developments that we have discussed are being built one village at a time, and as a consequence the developers will be able to revamp as they go along.

It is again appropriate to cite the eighteenth century. Reading Sir John Summerson's *Georgian London,* one is struck with how sophisticated some of the early planners were in the handling of large projects. Samuel Pepys Cockerell, who supervised the subdivision of the Foundling Hospital's extensive holdings in the Bloomsbury area, is a good example. Here are the guidelines he laid down; the master plan should embrace housing units for *all* classes: the focal points should be the residential squares and their gardens; the projects should be planned so that their edges blend with the existing neighborhoods; the plan should be amenable to step-by-step development so "that each part may be complete in itself and not dependent for its success and a return of profit to the undertakers upon the execution of the others." This was in 1790. One hundred and seventy four years later we are diligently copying the externals of eighteenth century planning. Maybe we should copy the fundamentals.

A<small>T</small> the conclusion of a report like this it is tempting to fob off unresolved questions by calling for more research. More research is always needed, but what is called for now most of all is simple observation. There is not a single approach that has not been

Patios at Baldwin Hills.

tried out on the ground, and the lessons are there for those who wish to look.

It's in new combinations of the old that the opportunity lies, and the moment was never better. Soon, perhaps, the mold will be set and what can seem so advanced today will be established as the status quo, and rigidly enforced by zoning boards and legislative rules and administrative regulations and the engineers, too. But this is why such a transitional period can be so stimulating. There is still time. The rules that will dictate the next great round of development haven't been written yet. The choices are still open.

APPENDIX A: TABULATION OF DEVELOPMENTS

These tabulations do not include all the projects that could qualify as cluster developments — and they include several that barely qualify. They do make up, however, a fairly sizeable cross-section of the most significant new developments in the U.S. and unless otherwise noted, the data is as of January 1, 1964.

For convenience, the developments have been divided into three groups — first, town houses developments; second, detached house developments; and third, "super" developments — large projects which are to include a variety of housing types, shopping centers, and the like. In all groups the order of listing is geographical: from north to south and from east to west.

Because of the wide variation in developers' terminology we have had to be somewhat inexact in describing multiple dwelling units. Generally, we have used "town house" for row units in which occupancy is top to bottom, rental or sale; "garden apartment" for rental units where occupancy may be only for one floor, and where there may be a common entry for two or more units.

The basic density figures are based upon the total acreage of the project. Acreage figures given for common open space do not include streets or parking areas, nor do they include land given for school or church sites.

Where only one section of a large project has been or is being built, figures are given for this part. Estimated data for the total project are included also but it is the first sections that are significant; very large developments tend to proceed a village at a time, and how many and what kind of houses will actually be built later is rather conjectural.

In the column on market response we have noted where pertinent the type of financing and the section of the 1961 Housing Act that applies, for the financing in many cases has had as much to do with sales success or lack of it as the cluster layout. Sales figures are not for "selling sales" but completed transactions in which the buyer has received mortgage approval.

TOWN HOUSES: CITY

DEVELOPMENT	DEVELOPER	SITE PLANNERS, ARCHITECTS	ACREAGE RAW LAND COST
LIBERTY SQUARE Liberty & Spring Street New Haven, Conn. Town house cooperative in redevelopment area Completed 1963	Urban Associates, Inc. 100 York Street New Haven, Conn. Gerald Diamond, Pres. James Linehan, Vice-Pres. Tel: 203 562-9997	Carl Koch & Associates, Inc. 55 Brattle Street Cambridge 38, Mass. Tel: 617 864-9212	1.9 acres $8,000 per acre
FAIRWAY GARDENS Eastern, Clifton & Russell Street New Haven, Conn. Duplex units; relocation project Completed 1962	Urban Associates, Inc. do.	Carl Koch & Associates, Inc. do.	5.4 acres $10,000 to 12,000 per acre
QUINNIPIAC GARDENS Quinnipiac Avenue New Haven, Conn. Duplex units; relocation project Completed 1963	Urban Associates, Inc. do.	Carl Koch & Associates, Inc. do.	3.9 acres $10,000 to 12,000 per acre
MORRELL PARK Academy & Red Lion Roads Philadelphia, Pa. Town house village in large, city-planned tract Construction began 1959 1500 units completed Dec. 1963	(Leonard) Gelman and (Paul) Curcillo 560 Church Road Elkins Park Philadelphia 7, Pa. Tel: 215 224-2391	Far Northeast master plan: City Planning Commission Penn Square Building Philadelphia 7, Pa. Edmund N. Bacon, Exec. Dir. Tel: 215 564-0744	354 acres $15,000 to 17,000 per acre
UNIVERSITY MEWS Spruce Street at 45th Philadelphia, Pa. Town houses around brick common 15 units completed Dec. 1963	(Maurice) Hertzfeld and (Irwin) Horowitz Assoc. 133 South 36th Street Philadelphia 4, Pa. Tel: 215 382-5400	Ronald C. Turner 249 South 24th Street Philadelphia, Pa. Tel: 215 563-5078	1.3 acres $75,000 per acre
RIVER PARK 4th, N,O, and Delaware Ave., S.W. Washington, D.C. Town houses and tower; redevelopment project Completed 1963	Reynolds Metals Company Sales: Foundation for Cooperatve Housing, Inc. 1001 Fifteenth Street, N.W. Washington, D.C. Edw. A. Burgoon, Vice-Pres. Tel: 202-393-5464	Charles M. Goodman, Assoc. 814 18th Street, N.W. Washington, D.C. Tel: 202-393-4863	11 acres $76,230 per acre

TY	OPEN SPACE AND RECREATIONAL FACILITIES		OWNERSHIP AND MAINTENANCE	PARKING	PRICE AND MARKET RESPONSE
its in 8 ildings	**Private:**	20' x 20' unfenced yards	Cooperative	Courts	Cooperative (FHA 221 d 3) $13,000 2 Bedroom $15,000 4 Bedroom
	Common:	½ acre, includes common greens, reflecting pool and play areas	Monthly charges include $11 for open space maintenance		
its per acre					Sold out before completion
nits in 22 uildings	**Private:**	20' x 20' fenced patios	Rental management	Courts	Rentals (FHA 221 d 3) $87.50 2 Bedroom $99.00 3 Bedroom
	Common:	2 acre common greens			
units per acre					Fully rented by completion
its in 16 uildings	**Private:**	20' x 20' fenced patios	Rental management	Courts	Rentals (FHA 221 d 3) $84.00 2 Bedroom $96.00 3 Bedroom
	Common:	1.5 acre common greens			
its per acre					Fully rented by completion
units	**Private:**	18' x 35' (min.) rear yards and small front yards	City Park Commission owns and maintains park areas	Garage in unit	Prices (FHA 203 b) $10,990 3 Bedroom (18') $12,350 3 Bedroom (20')
	Common:	30 acres, mostly wooded area along streams			(some units are rentals at $99 to $110)
nits per acre					All completed units sold and occupied as of Dec. 1963
its	**Private:**	16' x 17' fenced patios	Court consists of portions of lots, with maintenance up to each owner. All owners have access easement to court	Garage in unit	Prices $22,000 2 Bedroom $29,500 4 Bedroom
	Common:	90' x 50' brick common			
its per acre					Sales began May 1963 20 units sold as of Dec. 1963
nits: own houses ower units	**Private:**	16' x 20' walled gardens	Cooperative	Courts	Prices (FHA 213) Town houses: $22,000 2 Bedroom $29-31,000 4 Bedroom
	Common:	30,000 sq. ft., includes paved courts, swimming pool, playgrounds, sundecks on towers	Monthly charges include $11 to $30 for open space maintenance		Tower units: $17-20,000 2 Bedroom
its per acre					All town houses and 60% of tower units sold before completion; all sold by July 1963

DEVELOPMENT	DEVELOPER	SITE PLANNERS, ARCHITECTS	ACREAGE RAW LAND COST
CAPITOL PARK 4th Street, S.W. Washington, D.C. Town houses and towers; redevelopment project. 81 town houses, 4 towers completed and 318 town houses under construction as of Dec. 1963.	James H. Scheuer 4 West 58th Street New York 19, N. Y. Tel: 212-355-4100 Co-sponsors: H. R. H. Construction Corp. 300 G Street S.W. Washington, D.C. Tel: 202-783-8277	Chlothiel W. Smith & Assoc. 1056 Thomas Jefferson St., N.W. Washington, D.C. Tel: 202-338-7440	31.15 acres $78,000 per acre
CROSS KEYS Falls Road Baltimore, Maryland Town houses and towers with village center. Construction of town houses began Sept. 1963. First units to open Spring 1964.	Community Research and Development, Inc. 14 West Saratoga Street Baltimore 1, Maryland James W. Rouse, President Tel: 301-727-5502	Site plan: Richard Stauffer Staff architect, C. R. D. Inc. Associates: Collins & Kronstadt 706 Spring St. Silver Spring, Maryland Tel: 301-587-8642	68 acres $25,000 per acre
HARTSHORN HOMES Leigh Street and Kinney Richmond, Virginia Town houses around commons in redevelopment project Completed 1962	Reynolds Metals Co., Inc. and Viking Development Corp. of Richmond	Site plan: Harland Bartholomew Assoc. 815 17th Street, N.W. Washington, D.C. Tel: 202-347-9293 Architect: W. B. van Bakergem 102 East Cary Street Richmond, Va. Tel: 703-644-6568	10 acres $4,825 per acre
COLONIAL PARK 34th Street at Young Avenue Louisville, Kentucky Town houses around commons; redevelopment project Construction began 1962 104 units completed Dec. 1963	(Jesse) Bollinger and (George) Martin Inc. 300 West Main Street Louisville 2, Kentucky Tel: 502-583-0633 Equitable Properties, Inc. 8 East Long Street Columbus, Ohio Tel: 614-224-9171	Site plan: Miller, Wihry and Brooks 108 South 4th Street Louisville 2, Kentucky Tel: 502-583-5366 Architects: E. W. Augustus and John Doumas Saint Matthews, Kentucky Tel: 502-897-2488	34 acres $14,731 per acre (developed)

TY	OPEN SPACE AND RECREATIONAL FACILITIES		OWNERSHIP AND MAINTENANCE	PARKING	PRICE AND MARKET RESPONSE
units: town houses units in 5 towers ts per acre	**Private:** **Common:**	10′ x 20′ lawn area 9 acres, includes common greens, swimming pools, playgrounds, sundecks on towers	Rental management	Courts	Rentals: $180-195 Town houses: $180-195 2 Bedroom $225-245 3 Bedroom $115-275 Tower units All completed town houses rented (55 prior to completion), and first two towers 100% rented. Two other towers 85% rented as of Dec. 1963
units: town houses tower units ts per acre	**Private:** **Common:**	20′ x 25′ gardens 35 acres, to include walkways, lake, picnic areas and two recreation centers, each with swimming pool, tennis courts and club house	Rental management	Courts	Rentals: Town houses: $285 2 Bedroom $385 3 Bedroom
s acre	**Private:** **Common:**	20′ x 40′ front yards 30′ x 40′ rear yards 3.4 acres, includes common greens, swimming pool	Homeowners association Monthly assessment: $4	Courts	Prices (FHA 220) $10,950 3 Bedroom Sales began spring 1962: 28 remained to be sold June 1963. Final sales completed October 1963
its acre	**Private:** **Common:**	10′ x 15′ patios 8½ acres, includes common greens, proposed swimming pool and clubhouse	Homeowners association Monthly assessment: $5	Courts	Prices (FHA 221-d-2) $ 8,500 2 Bedroom $12,000 4 Bedroom Rentals (FHA 221-d-3) $59 2 Bedroom 82 houses sold (plus 22 pending financing approval) as of December 1963. Remaining 376 units to be rentals.

DEVELOPMENT	DEVELOPER	SITE PLANNERS, ARCHITECTS	ACREAGE RAW LAND COST
DUDLEY SQUARE Between Creswell & Highland Aves. Shreveport, Louisiana	N. O. Thomas, Jr. 2005 Henry C. Beck Building Shreveport, Louisiana	Somdal, Smitherman and Sorenson, Assoc. 1612 Fairfield Avenue Shreveport, Louisiana	2 acres $37,500 per acre
Town houses in walled enclave Completed 1959	Tel: 318-422-3189	Tel: 318-425-7721	
EAST HILLS PARK Frankstown and Vernon Roads Pittsburgh, Pennsylvania	Action Housing, Inc. (Sponsor) No. 1 Gateway Center Pittsburgh 22, Pa. Bernard Loshbough, Director Tel: 412-471-1014 Roland Catarinella 901 Elizabeth Street Pittsburgh, Pennsylvania Tel: 412-271-6407	Site plan: Simonds & Simonds 100 Ross Street Pittsburgh 19, Pa. 412-261-3808 Houses: B. Kenneth Johnstone and Assoc. Law and Finance Building Pittsburgh, Pa. Tel: 412-281-3040 Consultants: Satterlee and Smith	30 acres (initial secti $4,500 per acre for 131 acres
Town houses around commons First stage of a project for 1400 units. Construction began 1962 110 town houses completed,			
PARK TOWNE 5500 Lucas & Hunt Road St. Louis, Missouri	Wilbur R. Rosenblum 4511 Forest Park, Suite 206 St. Louis, Mo.	Architect: J. Richard Shelley 4311 East 7th Street Long Beach 4, Calif.	19 acres $12,000 per acre
Town houses around commons Completed 1961	Tel: 314-382-0602	Tel: 213-439-0908	
GENEVA TERRACE Schwerin Street between Sunnydale and Velasco Avenues San Francisco, California	Eichler Homes 2151 Saint Francis Drive Palo Alto, California Edward Eichler, President	Site plan and houses: Claude Oakland 111 New Montgomery Street San Francisco 5, Calif. Tel: 415-982-4575 Landscape: Royston, Hanamoto, Mayes & Beck 555 Clay Street San Francisco 11, California	21.5 acres $86,000 per acre
Town houses around commons 134 units completed, Dec. 1963	Tel: 415-321-1720	San Francisco 11, California Tel: 415-397-0594	

	OPEN SPACE AND RECREATION FACILITIES	OWNERSHIP AND MAINTENANCE	PARKING	PRICE AND MARKET RESPONSE
cre	**Private:** 31' x 30' patios **Common:** 600' x 150' to 95' common greens	Homeowners association Monthly assessment: $40	Central Garage	Prices $35,000 to $50,000 All sold. (14 sold before construction began in May 1958, other 6 sold within 7 months).
ts per acre	**Private:** 18' x 15' fenced patios **Common:** 15 acres, includes common greens, woods, ball field, playgrounds	Homeowners association (Portion of woods may be dedicated as city park) Monthly assessment: $10	Courts	Prices (FHA 203) $12,350 2 Bedroom $16,500 3 Bedroom Rentals: $89.50-100.00 1 Bedroom 78 units sold and 36 rented as of December 1963
ts its per acre	**Private:** 8' x 12' walled gardens **Common:** 9.8 acres, includes common greens, swimming pools, recreation building, playgrounds	Rental management	Courts	Rentals: $106 1 Bedroom $187 3 Bedroom 100% rented by opening date
its s per acre	**Private:** 18' x 22' fenced patios **Common:** 6.2 acres, includes common greens, swimming pool, playgrounds	Homeowners association Monthly assessment: $10	Courts	Prices (FHA 203) $27,950 4 Bedroom $29,950 4 Bedroom Sales began September 1962 100 units sold as of Dec. 1963

DEVELOPMENT	DEVELOPER	SITE PLANNERS, ARCHITECTS	ACREAGE RAW LAND CO$
HUNTINGTON CONTINENTAL Brookhurst and Adams Avenue Huntington Beach, California Town houses around commons Construction began 1963 445 units completed Dec. 1963	Kaufman and Broad Building Co. 3033 North Central Avenue Phoenix, Arizona Tel: 602-264-4306	Architects: Earl G. Kaltenbach, Inc. 9772 Katella Ave. Anaheim, Calif. Tel: 714-772-3361	52 acres $30,000 per acre
VISTA BAHIA Del Mar and Tustin Avenue Newport Beach Orange County, California Town houses around commons Completed 1963	Resplan Jack W. Mullan Don Woodward H. W. Wilson 428 32nd Street Newport Beach, Calif. Tel: 714-673-9420	Site plan: Jack W. Mullan 428 32nd Street Newport Beach, Calif. Architect: J. Richard Shelley 4311 East 7th Street Long Beach 4, Calif. Tel: 213-439-0908	4.9 acres $30,000 per acre

TOWN HOUSES: SUBURBAN

DEVELOPMENT	DEVELOPER	SITE PLANNERS, ARCHITECTS	ACREAGE RAW LAND COS
GEORGETOWN SOUTH Routes 28 & 234 Manassas, Virginia Town houses around commons Construction began Jan. 1963 250 units completed Dec. 1963 300 units under construction	Merit Developers 1845 Summit Place, N.W. Washington 9, D.C. D. Jay Hyman Lee G. Rubenstein Tel: 202-232-7300	Site plan and houses: Bagley and Soule & Assoc. Chevy Chase, Md. Tel: 301-652-5700	80 acres $5,000 per acre
HEATHER HILLS Hite Ave. North of Brownsboro Road Louisville, Kentucky Town houses with commons Construction began 1962 49 units completed Dec. 1963	The Kendall Company 4406 Shelbyville Road Louisville, Kentucky Joseph Cambron Tel: 502-895-3441	Site plan and houses: E. W. Augustus and John Doumas 135 Breckenridge Lane St. Matthews, Ky. Tel: 502-897-2488	9 acres $5,000 per acre

	OPEN SPACE AND RECREATIONAL FACILITIES		OWNERSHIP AND MAINTENANCE	PARKING	PRICE AND MARKET RESPONSE	
s	Private:	20' x 40' fenced patios	Homeowners association	1 detached garage per unit	Prices (FHA 203-B)	
					$ 9,990	1 Bedroom
	Common:	22 acres, includes common greens, 2 swimming pools, 1 recreation building	Monthly assessment: $12	plus courts	$11,990	2 Bedroom
					$14,990	4 Bedroom
ts per acre					Sales began Spring 1963; 445 units sold, 306 pending, as of Dec. 1963	
	Private:	26' x 15' fenced patios	Homeowners association	2 detached garages per unit	Prices:	
					$28,500	2 Bedroom
	Common:	2.5 acres, includes large putting green, 2 swimming pools	Monthly assessment: $35		$38,500	3 Bedroom
per acre					Sales began Nov. 1962 All units sold by Oct. 1963	

	OPEN SPACE AND RECREATIONAL FACILITIES		OWNERSHIP AND MAINTENANCE	PARKING	PRICE AND MARKET RESPONSE	
ts grouped blocks of to 90	Private:	18' x 17' front yards 18' x 25' rear yards	Developers, pending formation of homeowners association	Courts	Prices (FHA 203)	
					$11,490	2 Bedroom
					$14,990	3 Bedroom
	Common:	20 acres, includes common greens, park, playgrounds	Monthly assessment: $3			
per acre					Sales began April 1963. 205 units sold as of Dec. 1963	
	Private:	18' x 30' fenced patios	Homeowners association	Courts	Prices (FHA 203) $12,500 to $14,600	
			Monthly assessment: $3			
	Common:	1 acre, includes swimming pool and small park (on edge of development)			Sales began November 1962 50 units sold as of Dec. 1963	
per acre						

DEVELOPMENT	DEVELOPER	SITE PLANNERS, ARCHITECTS	ACREAGE RAW LAND CO
CREEKSIDE 1470 Creekside Drive Walnut Creek, California	The Duffel-Smoot Companies Joe B. Smoot, Inc. 3696 Mount Diablo Boulevard Lafayette, California	Site plan and houses: Larry Freels 28 Los Serros Avenue Walnut Creek, Calif. Tel: 415-935-3485	7.5 acres $50,000 per acre
Town houses around common courts Completed 1962	Tel: 415-254-4308 415-283-0900	Collaborators: Robert Greenlee, Walter Lucas, F. E. Kupper, and Carl Wisser	
POMEROY GREEN Benton Street and Pomeroy Ave. Santa Clara, California	Eichler Homes 2151 St. Francis Drive Palo Alto, California Edward Eichler, President	Site plan and houses: Claude Oakland 111 New Montgomery Street San Francisco 5, California Tel: 415-982-4575 Landscape: Royston, Hanamoto, Mayes & Beck 555 Clay Street San Francisco 11, California	7.5 acres $12,000 per acre
Town houses around commons Completed 1962	Tel: 415-321-1720	Tel: 415-397-0594	
TERRACE AT PEACOCK GAP Biscayne Drive Marin Bay San Rafael, California Strip of town houses bordering golf course. Completed 1962	Weldwood Structures Division of U.S. Plywood Corp. 1450 Doolittle Drive San Leandro, California Warner R. Odenthal, Genl. Mgr. Tel: 415-562-6500	Architect: Sherrill Broudy 1000 Coast Village Road Santa Barbara, California Tel: 805-969-0816	1.5 acres $50,000 per acre

ITY	OPEN SPACE AND RECREATIONAL FACILITIES		OWNERSHIP AND MAINTENANCE	PARKING	PRICE AND MARKET RESPONSE
nits	**Private:**	15′ x 12′ fenced patios	Homeowners association	Courts	Prices (condominium)
					$12,650 1 Bedroom
	Common:	3.7 acres, includes four courts, each with own swimming pool	Monthly assessment: $35		$21,500 3 Bedroom
					Rentals:
					$110-130 1 Bedroom
					$150-170 2 Bedroom
units per acre					All 148 rental units rented before completion. All 46 condominium units sold as of December 1963
its in 5 buildings	**Private:**	10′ x20′ fenced patios	Cooperative	Courts	Prices (FHA 213)
					$21,410 4 Bedroom
	Common:	2.4 acres, includes common greens, swimming pool, recreation center	Monthly assessment: $32		
its per acre					Sales began Jan. 1962; all units sold by July 1963
its	**Private:**	Small terrace, balcony, or 13½′ x 17′ atriums	Homeowners association	Garage in unit	Prices (condominium)
					$25,900 2 Bedroom, 2 story
	Common:	small common greens with swimming pool	Monthly assessment: $39		$27,900 2 Bedroom, atrium
					Sales began spring 1962
					15 sold by September 1962
its per acre					Last one sold January 1963

DETACHED HOUSE DEVELOPMENTS

DEVELOPMENT	DEVELOPER	SITE PLANNERS, ARCHITECTS	ACREAGE RAW LAND COST
THE HIGHLANDS Pumpkin Hill Road Ledyard, Connecticut 250 houses completed Dec. 1963	Lifetime Homes Inc. 523 Boston Post Road Old Saybrook, Connecticut George J. Achenbach, Pres. Curtis Sykora, Vice Pres. Tel: 203-388-3411	Site plan: James Frost Technical Planning Associates 37 Whitney Avenue New Haven, Conn. Tel: 203-787-1213 Architect: Robert Wendler 415 Temple Street New Haven, Conn. Tel: 203-624-9959	450 acres $450 per acre
SUNRISE Guilford, Connecticut Conventional development with common green. 47 houses completed Dec. 1963	Macauley Development Co., Inc. Horseshoe Road Guilford, Connecticut Irving P. Macauley, President John Macauley, Vice President Tel: 203-453-2383	Site plan: John Macauley and Hugh Jones Whitefield Street Guilford, Conn. Tel: 203-453-5216	123 acres $900 per acre
THE WOODLANDS Farmington, Connecticut Construction of apartments began 1964; houses held up pending resolution of water distribution problem.	Howard L. Menzel Red Oak Hill Farmington, Conn. Tel: 203-677-0465	Site plan: Merrill H. Lincoln Technical Planning Associates 37 Whitney Avenue New Haven, Conn. Tel: 203-787-1213	145 acres $1,000 per acre
VILLAGE GREEN Route 206 Hillsborough, New Jersey Completed 1963	(Sidney) Halpern— (Seymour) Tuschak Agency 15 West Main Street Somerville, New Jersey Tel: 201-722-3400 Melvin Konwiser P.O. Box 898 Union, New Jersey	Site plan: William E. Roach, Jr. Planning Director Somerset County Planning Board Somerville, New Jersey Tel: 201-725-4700 And Robert Catlin & Associates Rockaway, New Jersey Tel: 201-627-3929	79 acres $1,000 per acre
BRUNSWICK ACRES Finnegans Lane & Franklin Park Road South Brunswick, New Jersey Construction to begin 1964	Yenom Corporation 12 Central Street Metuchen, New Jersey Kenneth Berg, President Tel: 201-548-5700	Site plan: H. Thomas Carr 90 Smith Street Perth Amboy, New Jersey Tel: 201-442-9292	235 acres
PARKWOOD N.C. Highway #54 Lowes Grove North Carolina 281 houses completed 1963	Kavanagh-Smith & Co. First Southern Building Greensboro, North Carolina Roger Kavanagh, Pres. Tel: 919-273-2521	Site plan: Willard C. Byrd & Associates 270 Peachtree Building Atlanta 3, Georgia Tel: 404-524-4532	560 acres $680 per acre

NSITY	OPEN SPACE AND RECREATIONAL FACILITIES		OWNERSHIP AND MAINTENANCE	PARKING	PRICE AND MARKET RESPONSE
ouses ...... its per acre	**Private:** 100' x 150' lots **Common:** 40 acres, includes 10-acre lake, playgrounds, walkways and (proposed) beach club & tennis courts		Developers, pending formation of home-owners association. Developer retains $100 from each house sold to cover costs until transfer of control	Garage with house	Prices $15,500 to $21,500 Sales began April 1962 with pre-opening deposits on 80 houses. 273 houses sold as of December 1963
ouses ...... per acre	**Private:** 20,000 sq. ft. lots **Common:** 5 acres, includes common greens, (proposed) a small boat marina		Homeowners association Monthly assessment: $1	Garage with house	Prices: $22,000 to $36,500 Sales began 1961. All com-completed houses sold.
ouses arden apart-ment units ...... its per acre	**Private:** 125' x 240' sq. ft. lots **Common:** 30 acres, includes woods and park strips weaving throughout area.		To be dedicated to town for 35 years	Garage with house	Prices: $30,000 to $50,000 Rentals: $165 to $200
uses ...... per acre	**Private:** 15,000 sq. ft. lots (min.) **Common:** 42 acres, includes large commons, woods, baseball diamonds		Dedicated to municipality	Garage with house	Prices: $19,000 to $21,000 Sales began August 1962 All houses sold by Feb. 1963
ouses ...... its per acre	**Private:** 85' x 120' lots **Common:** 25 acres, to include park, small play lots, baseball diamonds, bath and tennis club		Dedicated to municipality (Beach and tennis club to be owned and managed by developer)	Garage with house	Prices: $19,000 to $24,000
ouses ...... its per acre	**Private:** 85' x 150' lots **Common:** 146 acres, includes 35-acre lake, park strips between clusters		Homeowners association Annual assessment: $18	Garage with house	Prices: $13,000 to $22,000 278 houses sold as of December 1963

DEVELOPMENT	DEVELOPER	SITE PLANNERS, ARCHITECTS	ACREAGE RAW LAND COST
SEA PINES PLANTATION Hilton Head Island South Carolina Construction began 1957; inn, golf course and 97 houses completed Dec. 1963	Sea Pines Plantation Co. Hilton Head Island South Carolina Charles Fraser, President Tel: 803-785-3333	Site plan: Sasaki & Walker Assoc. 23 Main Street Watertown, Mass. Tel: 617-926-1106 Custom houses designed by: John Wade and McGinty, Stanley, Corkern & Wiggins of Sea Pines Plantation Co.	5,200 acres $310 per acre
GEORGETOWN EAST Woodland, off Highway 57 Cedarburg, Wisconsin Construction of first 50 houses began 1963. 6 completed Dec. 1963	(Clarence) Dittmar Homes, Inc. P.O. Box 129 Menomonee Falls, Wisc. Tel: 414-781-3330 Cedarburg Development Co., Inc. Paul Binzak 840 North 3rd Street Milwaukee, Wisconsin Tel: 414-272-2855	Site plan: William L. Nelson & Associates 1733 North Farwell Avenue Milwaukee 2, Wisconsin Tel: 414-271-1862 Houses: Ray Prell & Assoc. 12255 W. Burleigh Avenue Milwaukee, Wisconsin Tel: 414-786-8820	70 acres $800 to 1,000 per acre
VILLE DU PARC South of Highland Road Mequon, Wisconsin 18-hole golf course and model houses completed Dec. 1963	The Ville du Parc Company 8828 North Port Washington Rd. Milwaukee 17, Wisconsin Harris Evans, Pres. Tel: 414-352-5121	Site Plan: William L. Nelson & Associates do.	600 acres $2,500 per acre (1963 appraised value)
LAKESIDE HILLS Lewis & Clark Highway St. Louis County Missouri Construction began 1963 8 houses completed Dec. 1963	Keeney-Toelle Real Estate Co. 5500 Natural Bridge Avenue St. Louis 20, Missouri Eugene W. Sutherland, Sr. Tel: 314-385-7370	Site plan: George W. Kropp & Associates Clayton 5, Missouri Tel: 314-725-7493 Houses: Paul Coleman 1205 Lynn Gate Kirkwood, Missouri Tel: 314-966-4514	90 acres $2,100 per acre
LOMA VISTA 88th Terrace & Blue Ridge Boulevard Kansas City, Missouri Detached houses and rental units Construction to begin 1964	c/o Byers Construction Company 1006 Grand Avenue Kansas City, Missouri George Byers Reed Byers Tel: 816-842-0297	Site plan: Hugh King and Associates 3601 Main Street Kansas City, Kansas Tel: 816-753-3320	42 acres $3,000 per acre

SITY	OPEN SPACE AND RECREATIONAL FACILITIES		OWNERSHIP AND MAINTENANCE	PARKING	PRICE AND MARKET RESPONSE
ouses	**Private:**	100' x 100' to 100' x 200' lots	Developer owns and maintains under contractual arrangement with homeowners	Garage with house	Prices: $20,000 to $75,000 houses $ 3,500 to $20,000 lots
	Common:	125-acre golf course, 1,600-acre wildlife preserve and 3½ miles of beach, trails, and 50' walkway easements	Annual assessment averages: $50		
per 3.5 acres					Lot sales began 1957 450 lots sold as of Dec. 1963
ouses	**Private:**	8,000 sq. ft. lots	Parks to be dedicated to municipality	Garage with house	Prices: $19,000 to $23,500
	Common:	10 acres, includes common greens and small parks linked by pedestrian ways			
its per acre					Sales began July 1963 17 houses sold as of December 1963
ouses	**Private:**	10,000 sq. ft. lots	Golf course owned by Parcwood Country Club, Inc.	Courts	Prices: $35,000 to $50,000
	Common:	440 acres, includes small common areas, 27-hole golf course on 205 acres, swimming pool, fishing pond, riding stable, bridle trails, walkways and park along river	Homeowners association owns rest Monthly assessment: $10		
per acre					Sales to begin 1964
ouses	**Private:**	80' x 150' lots	Homeowners association	Garage with house	Prices: $22,000 to $30,000
	Common:	18 acres, includes 1½-acre lake, woods playground & picnic area			
its per acre					Sales began 1963 5 houses sold as of December 1963
nits: etached houses ental units n 33 bldgs.	**Private:**	75' x 120' house lots	Developer will own and maintain	Garage with detached house	Prices: $18,000 to $25,000 Rentals: $95 to $125
	Common:	12 acres, to include swimming pool and bath house	Monthly assessment: $4	Courts for other units	
nits per acre					Sales to begin Summer 1964

Development	DEVELOPER	SITE PLANNERS ARCHITECTS	ACREAGE RAW LAND CO
FOUR SEASONS Woodsmill Road & Olive Street Road St. Louis, Missouri	New Four Seasons, Inc. Box 308, Route 2 Chesterfield, Missouri Sidney Kandel, President	Site plan: Harland Bartholomew & Assoc. 815 17th Street N.W. Washington, D.C.	138 acres $4,000 per acre
Detached houses, rental units and shopping center. 125 units completed Dec. 1963	Tel: 314-469-3010	Tel: 202-347-9293	
HAMPDEN HEIGHTS Hampden Avenue, Havana & Yosemite Denver, Colorado	Dream House Builders Co. 1402 Denver U.S. National Center Denver, Colorado Benjamin Elenbogen, Pres.	Site plan: Harman, O'Donnell & Henninger, Associates Second & Detroit St. Denver 6, Colorado	347 acres $3,500 per acre
150 units completed Dec. 1963	Tel: 303-266-0636	Tel: 303-388-4228	

SUPER DEVELOPMENTS

DEVELOPMENT	DEVELOPER	SITE PLANNERS, ARCHITECTS	ACREAGE RAW LAND CO
NEW SEABURY **BRIGHT COVES VILLAGE** Mashpee Traffic Circle (Routes 28 & 151) Waquoit, Massachusetts	Emil Hanslin Associates, Inc. 820 Lynn Fells Parkway Melrose, Massachusetts	Site plan: George E. Hayes, Associates 101 Atamont Avenue Melrose, Massachusetts Tel: 617-665-0427	3,000 acres Bright Coves: 128 ac
First of eleven villages planned. Construction began 1960; 59 houses completed Dec. 1963	Tel: 617-665-2323 Cape Cod: 617-428-6992	Houses: Royal Barry Wills; Robert Woods Kennedy; Bedar and Alpers; Robert Damora	
CROFTON Route 3 & Route 450 Anne Arundel County Maryland	Crofton Corporation (Subsidiary of Crawford Corp.) 1707 H. Street, N.W. Washington, D.C.. W. H. Crawford, President	Site plan: Mott and Hayden 908 20th Street, N.W. Washington, D.C. Tel. 202-337-6472	1,500 acres $2,500 per acre
Satellite community with residential, commercial, industrial and recreational centers. Construction of recreational facilities, first houses, began 1963; 6 model houses completed December 1963	Carl Norcross, Vice President Tel: 202-298-6560	Architects: Macomber and Peter 1611 Connecticut Ave., N.W. Washington, D.C. Tel: 202-234-4359	

Y	RECREATIONAL FACILITIES OPEN SPACES AND		OWNERSHIP AND MAINTENANCE	PARKING	PRICE AND MARKET RESPONSE
ts ached houses tal units 0 buildings	**Private:**	12,000 sq. ft. lots 12′ x 8′ balconies for other units	Homeowners association Monthly assessment: $40	Garage with house and other units	Prices: $26,200 to $35,500 Rentals: $139 to $295
s per acre	**Common:**	47 acres, includes golf course, swimming pool, club house			42 houses sold as of Dec. 1963
uses	**Private:**	9,000 to 10,400 sq. ft. lots	Park area adjoining school dedicated to municipality	Garage with house plus off street visitor parking	Prices: $21,000 to $25,900
per acre	**Common:**	36.5 acres, includes central commons with park and recreation bldg, green strip along pipe-line easement	Homeowners association owns rest Annual assessment $25		Sales began 1962. 146 houses sold as of December 1963

SITY	OPEN SPACE AND RECREATIONAL FACILITITES		OWNERSHIP AND MAINTENANCE	PARKING	PRICE AND MARKET RESPONSE
etached ouses	**Private:**	8,788 to 35,000 sq. ft. lots	Developer, pending formation of home-owners association	Garage with house	Prices: $14,400 to $35,000: houses $ 3,000 to $15,200: lots
its per acre	**Common:**	33 acres, includes beach, seven common docks			
project: 3,750 or 1.2 units cre)		Of total 3,000 acres, 1,770 are to be common)	Annual assessment: $50		Sales began September 1962 72 houses and 147 lots sold as of December 1963
units: detached houses town houses rental units	**Private:**	80′ x 120′ to 100′ x 150′ house lots 20′ x 24′ town house patios	Developer to own and operate golf and country club; membership voluntary	Garage with house Courts for other units	Prices: $20,000 to $35,000: houses
s per acre	**Common:**	300 acres, to include: village green, 210-acre golf course, swimming pool, lakes, tennis courts			

DEVELOPMENT	DEVELOPER	SITE PLANNERS, ARCHITECTS	ACREAGE RAW LAND CC
AMERICANA FAIRFAX U.S. Route 413 and Little River Tpke. Annandale Fairfax County, Virginia	Carl M. Freeman Associates 1111 Fidler Lane Silver Spring, Maryland	Site plan: S. E. Sanders and Associates 1908 K. Street N.W. Washington 6, D.C. Tel: 202-338-0554	260 acres $20,000 per acre (1963 appraised val
Garden apartment complex with town houses and tower. Construction began 1961 1,000 units completed Dec. 1963	Tel: 301-588-5522	Buildings designed by staff architects of Carl M. Freeman Assoc.	
RESTON FIRST VILLAGE Outer Circumferential Hwy. & Rt. 606 Fairfax County, Virginia	Simon Enterprises 250 West 57th Street New York 19, New York Robert E. Simon, Jr.	Site plan: Whittlesey & Conklin 31 Union Square New York 3, N. Y. Tel: 212-924-4700	128 acres (first pha First Village)
Detached houses, town house clusters, towers and recreational facilities and commercial center in first of 7 planned communities. Construction began 1963; recreational facilities completed December 1963	Tel: 212-586-3670 Reston, Virginia Tel: 703-471-4430	Architects: Whittlesey & Conklin Charles M. Goodman Assoc. Satterlee & Smith Geddes, Brecher, Qualls and Cunningham.	(First Village: 700 a Reston: 6,810 acres
HUNTING CREEK U.S. 42 and Harrod's Creek Jefferson County, Kentucky	Paul Semonin Company Starks Building Louisville 2, Kentucky Tel: 502-584-2375	Site plan: Miller, Wihry and Brooks 108 South 4th Street Louisville 2, Ky. Tel: 502-583-5366	964 acres $2,000 per acre
Clusters of detached houses, town houses, rental units (plus lot sales) and commercial center. Construction of first section and golf course began 1963.	Owner: Hunting Creek Co., Inc. Louisville, Ky.	Architects (of country club): E. W. Augustus & John Doumas Saint Matthews, Kentucky Tel: 502-897-2488	
CHAPEL HILL Flakes Mill Road DeKalb County, Georgia	General Builders, Corp. 75 Cedar Street Babylon, New York Mr. Janis Risbergs, President	Site plan: Northern Properties, Inc. 25 West 43rd Street New York 36, New York Gerald Lloyd, President	1,079 acres $1,500 per acre
Clusters of detached houses, town houses, tower units and several commercial centers. Construction began 1963.	Tel: 516-669-3805	Tel: 212-695-5050	
WESTCHESTER U.S. 36 & Route 4 Springfield,Illinois	Westchester Trust Charles Johnson 526 East Capitol Street Springfield, Illinois	Site plan: Richard Selleg Assoc. 103 West Main Street St. Charles, Illinois	366 acres
Detached houses, town house clusters, and rental units near commercial center. Construction began 1963	Tel: 217-544-4671	Tel: 312-584-1212	

SITY	OPEN SPACE AND RECREATIONAL FACILITIES		OWNERSHIP AND MAINTENANCE	PARKING	PRICE AND MARKET RESPONSE

) units:
) town houses
) units in 72 buildings
) units in 1 tower
	Private:	10' x 20' terraces (some open, some partially fenced) for town houses; balconies or terraces for apartments	Rental management	Courts, central garage for tower	Rentals:
					$195 to $260
					   3 & 4 Bedroom town houses
					$110 to $190
					   1 & 3 Bedroom apartments

units per acre	**Common:**	68.5 acres, includes parks, picnic areas, tennis and basketball courts, 5 swimming pools			All completed units rented
units: detached houses town houses rental units units in 1 tower	**Private:**	8,000 to 18,000 sq ft. lots 21' x 25' or 28' x 14' town house gardens and patios	Homeowners association	Garage with house Courts for town houses and tower and one central, underground garage	Prices: $ 4,500 to $10,000: house lots $32,000: town houses (average) Rentals: $150 to $300 tower units
units per acre l project: 35 units, or units per acre)	**Common:**	31 acres, includes 30-acre lake, parks, common greens, tennis & swimming club (Of total 6,810 acres, 1,500 are to be common)	Annual assessment: $65 maximum for first three years; thereafter home-owners will be charged a percentage of assessed value of common areas.		Lot sales to begin December 1963; Town house sales Spring 1964
8 units: 9 detached houses 9 town houses 0 rental units	**Private:**	14,570 sq. ft. lots 25' x 60' town house patios or gardens	Developers, pending formation of home-owners asociation. Some areas to be deeded as public parks	Garage with detached house Courts for other units	Prices: $25,000 to $50,000: houses $18,000 to $22,000: town houses
units per acre	**Common:**	307 acres, to include 224-acre golf course, 80 acres of woodland with sledding hill, 3-acre central green. Also, club house, pool, tennis courts, riding club & boat club	Membership in Hunting Creek Country Club not restricted to residents, membership fee: $500; monthly dues: $25		Sales of houses to begin 1964
0 units: 0 detached houses 0 town houses 0 units in 2 towers	**Private:**	8,000 sq. ft. to 1½ acre lots 20' x 30' town house gardens	To be dedicated to county	Garage with detached house Courts for other units	Prices: $14,500 to $35,000 Rentals: $110 to $130
units per acre	**Common:**	207 acres, to include parks, bridle paths, stables, baseball fields and pond			Sales to begin 1964
8 units: 8 detached houses) town houses) rental units	**Private:**	65' x 120' to 90' x 150' house lots	To be deeded to Springfield Park District	Garage with detached house Courts for other units	Prices: $21,500 to $38,000: houses Rentals: $120 to $165: 1, 2 & 3 Bedroom
its per acre	**Common:**	18 acres, includes 6 small parks			

DEVELOPMENT	DEVELOPER	SITE PLANNERS, ARCHITECTS	ACREAGE RAW LAND COST
LAKEHURST W. Belleview Ave. & Kipling Street Denver, Colorado Detached houses around cul-de-sacs. Town houses & other units planned for Lakehurst section of 7,000-acre "Columbine Community." 52 houses completed Dec. 1963	Perlmutter Homes 4390 Santa Fe Englewood, Colorado David Perlmutter, President Tel: 303-761-1332	Site plan: Harman, O'Donnell & Henninger Associates, Inc. Second and Detroit St. Denver 6, Colorado Tel: 303-388-4228 Architects: Eugene Sternberg 2009 West Littleton Blvd. Littleton, Colorado Tel: 303-798-2565	75.6 acres (1st stage $1,800 per acre (Total Lakehurst projec 1,000 acres)
GREENHAVEN '70 Riverside Boulevard Sacramento, California Detached houses and rental units connected by park strip to commercial, cultural and recreational centers. 90 houses completed, 30 under construction Dec. 1963	Kermit L. Lincoln 3190 Old Tunnel Road Lafayette, California Tel: 415-935-7000 Harold E. Parker 3520 Golden Gateway Lafayette, California Tel: 415-284-7043	Site plan: David B. Whittet 261 Castle Hill Ranch Road Walnut Creek, California Tel: 415-935-0918	708 acres $5,000 per acre
EL DORADO HILLS U.S. 50, East of Sacramento Sacramento, California Park Village and Governor's Village are first of 12 villages planned. In Park Village, 93 houses completed and 34 under construction as of December 1963	El Dorado Hills West P.O. Box 1 El Dorado Hills, California Ronald C. Anderson, President Tel: 916-988-3441	Site plan: Victor Gruen and Associates 135 South Dohemy Drive Beverly Hills, California Tel: 213-274-7134 Architects: Anshen and Allen 461 Bush Street San Francisco, Calif. Tel: 415-986-6421	180 acres (Park Village $1,500 per acre (El Dorado Hills: 9,800 acres)
CARMEL VALLEY GOLF AND COUNTRY CLUB Carmel, California Clusters of detached houses, town houses and rental units.	Green Meadows, Inc. Edgar H. Haber, President Route 2, Box 651 Carmel, California Tel: 408-624-5323	Site plan and clubhouse: (Gordon) Hall and (Donald) Goodhue 380 Cannery Row Monterey, California Tel: 408-375-9595	245 acres $6,000 per acre
SKYLINE FOREST Skyline Drive off California Highway 1 Monterey, California Clusters of detached houses, town houses and rental units including one tower set against forested hillside. Construction began 1963	Monterey Peninsula Associates Wright S. Fisher, President 55 Soledad Drive Monterey, Calif. Tel: 408-373-2424	Site plan and houses: Hall and Goodhue do.	211 acres $4,000 to 7,500 per a (Estimated:)

SITY	OPEN SPACE AND RECREATION FACILITIES		OWNERSHIP AND MAINTENANCE	PARKING	PRICE AND MARKET RESPONSE
uses	**Private:**	9,000 sq. ft. lots	To be dedicated to municipality	Garage with house	Prices: $16,500 to $22,500
	Common:	8.6 acres of parks			
its per acre Lakehurst proj- 3,000 units, or ts per acre)		(of total 1,000 acres, 42.3 are to be common)			Sales began August 1963 and 80 houses sold as of Dec. 1963
units: detached houses rental units	**Private:**	6,300 to 10,000 sq. ft. lots	All open space, except swimming club, dedicated to municipality	Garage with house	Prices: $22,000 to $50,000 houses (includes $300 swimming club membership) Rentals: $100 to $250
	Common:	125 acres, includes parks, swimming and tennis clubs	Homeowners association owns swimming club. Monthly fee: $4		
its per acre					125 houses sold as of December 1963
Village) nits: etached houses ental units	**Private:**	90' x 140' lots	Public golf course	Garage with house	Prices: $22,000 to $26,000 houses
	Common:	36 acres, includes 11-acre park, Olympic swimming pool, baseball diamond, play ground & golf course	11-acre park deeded to community service district Annual assessment: $1 per $100 assessed valuation		
its per acre project: 0 units, or ts per acre)		(Of total 9,800 acres, 1,000 to 1,500 are to be common)			Sales began June 1963 90 houses sold as of Dec. 1963
units: detached houses town houses and rental units	**Private:**	10,000 to 12,000 sq. ft. lots 25' wide town house yards	Developer owns Carmel Valley Golf and Country Club (all residents will be members) Maintenance to be includ-ed in membership fee of $3,000 and monthly dues: $35	Garage with house Courts for other units	Prices: $40,000 to $60,000 houses
	Common:	153 acres, includes 130-acre golf course			
t per acre					
units: detached houses town houses tower and other rental units	**Private:**	7,000 to 15,000 sq. ft. lots 25' wide town house yards	Special service district maintenance Nominal monthly assessment (mostly forrested area)	Garage with house Courts for other units	Prices: $35,000 to $65,000 houses
	Common:	101 acres, includes common greens, 89-acre forest preserve, park & recreation club			
ts per acre					

APPENDIX B: NEW YORK STATE CLUSTER ENABLING ACT

This act, Chapter 963 of the Laws of 1963, clarifies the rights of
local governments to permit cluster development.

Section 281 of the town law. Approval of plats; conditions for changes in zoning provisions. The town board is hereby empowered by resolution to authorize the planning board, simultaneously with the approval of a plat or plats pursuant to this article, to modify applicable provisions of the zoning ordinance, subject to the conditions hereinafter set forth and such other reasonable conditions as the town board may in its discretion add thereto. Such authorization shall specify the lands outside the limits of any incorporated village to which this procedure may be applicable. The purposes of such authorization shall be to enable and encourage flexibility of design and development of land in such a manner as to promote the most appropriate use of land, to facilitate the adequate and economical provision of streets and utilities, and to preserve the natural and scenic qualities of open lands. The conditions hereinabove referred to are as follows:

(a) If the owner makes written application for the use of this procedure, it may be followed at the discretion of the planning board if, in said board's judgment, its application would benefit the town.

(b) This procedure shall be applicable only to lands zoned for residential purposes, and its application shall result in a permitted number of dwelling units which shall in no case exceed the number which could be permitted, in the planning board's judgment, if the land were subdivided into lots conforming to the minimum lot size and density requirements of the zoning ordinance applicable to the district or districts in which such land is situated and conforming to all other applicable requirements.

(c) The dwelling units permitted may be, at the discretion of the planning board and subject to the conditions set forth by the town board, in detached, semi-detached, attached, or multi-story structures.

(d) In the event that the application of this procedure results in a plat showing lands available for park, recreation, open space, or other municipal purposes directly related to the plat, then the planning board as a condition of plat approval may establish such conditions on the ownership, use, and maintenance of such lands as it deems necessary to assure the preservation of such lands for their intended purposes. The town board may require that such conditions shall be approved by the town board before the plat may be approved for filing.

(e) The proposed site plan, including areas within which structures may be located, the height and spacing of buildings, open spaces and their landscaping, off-street open and enclosed parking spaces, and streets, driveways and all other physical features as shown on said plan or otherwise described, accompanied by a statement setting forth the nature of such modifications, changes, or supplementations of existing zoning provisions as are not shown on said site plan, shall be subject to review and public hearing by the planning board in the same manner as set forth in sections two hundred seventy-six and two hundred seventy-seven of this article for the approval of plats.

(f) On the filing of the plat in the office of the county clerk or register, a copy shall be filed with the town clerk, who shall make appropriate notations and references thereto in the town zoning ordinance or map.

APPENDIX C: LOCAL ORDINANCES

1. Residential Planned Community Ordinance, Fairfax County, Virginia (Adopted July 18, 1962)

(A) PURPOSE AND INTENT

The RPC District (Residential Planned Community) is intended to permit in accordance with the master plan the development of planned satellite communities containing not less than 750 contiguous acres under one ownership or control in those areas of the County provided with sanitary sewers, sewage disposal facilities, adequate highway access and public water supply. Within such planned communities, the location of all residential, commercial, industrial and governmental uses, school sites, parks, playgrounds, recreation areas, parking areas and other open spaces shall be controlled in such a manner as to permit a variety of housing accommodations and land uses in orderly relationship to one another. Such planned communities, when approved, shall constitute a part of the master plan for the County as a whole, and the preliminary consideration of such planned communities by the Planning Commission shall be based on recognition of this requirement.

(B) PROCEDURE FOR ESTABLISHMENT

(1) Following approval of a satellite community as a part of the master plan of the County, the Board of County Supervisors may create within such planned location an RPC District containing a minimum land area of not less than 750 acres under one ownership or control. Additional land area may be added to an existing RPC District if it is adjacent or forms a logical addition to an existing RPC District. The procedure for an addition shall be the same as if an original application were filed, and all of the requirements of this article shall apply except the minimum acreage requirement of 750 acres.

(2) The applicant shall furnish with his application for rezoning 15 copies of a preliminary plan, prepared or certified by a surveyor or engineer duly authorized by the State to practice as such, showing the proposed general layout, the general location of the various types of land uses, the proposed densities of population in residential areas, a major thoroughfare plan, a public utility plan, a storm drainage plan and a plan showing the location of recreation spaces, parks, schools and other public or community uses.

(3) Following approval by the Planning Commission and the Board of County Supervisors of a preliminary plan, the applicant shall furnish 15 copies of a final plan of any section of not less than 100 acres of the land shown on the preliminary plan, prepared or certified by a surveyor or engineer duly authorized by the State to practice as such, showing the layout of all major and local thoroughfares and local streets, the location of all buildings, parking areas, pedestrian ways, utility easements, lot lines, open spaces, parks, recreation areas, school sites, playgrounds, the proposed use of all buildings and the metes and bounds of all dedicated areas and lots. The applicant shall also furnish a proposed deed of dedication including restrictions safeguarding the use of open spaces and preventing encroachment upon open spaces between buildings. The applicant shall furnish a deed, or deeds, to land determined by the County to be needed for public elementary and intermediate school purposes. When the final plan and deed of dedication shall have been approved by the Planning Commission as being in conformity with this section and with any changes or requirements of the Board of County Supervisors on the preliminary plan and it has been determined that the applicant has complied with the requirements of Chapter 23 of the Code of Fairfax County (which is the Subdivision Control Ordinance) whether or not it is a subdivision, it shall be approved for recordation and recorded. Thereafter, no modification may be made in any final plan except by an amended final plan submitted as provided for the original plan.

(C) PERMITTED POPULATION DENSITY

(1) Overall density

The overall population density shown on the master plan for development as an RPC District and associated industrial and commercial uses shall not exceed an average density of 11 persons per acre. In computing population density, a factor of 3.7 persons shall be used per one family dwelling, 3.0 persons per garden type apartment unit or town house and 1.5 persons per high rise apartment unit.

(2) Types of density

Three residential density areas shall be permitted in an RPC zone in the locations shown on the master plan. Such density areas shall be designated low, medium and high.

a. The population density within a low density area shall not exceed 3.8 persons per acre of gross residential area.

b. The population density within a medium density area shall not exceed 14 persons per acre of gross residential area.

c. The population density within a high density area shall not exceed 60 persons per acre of gross residential area.

(3) Computation of density

In computing average density on any final plan of a part of an RPC District, which district at the time of its creation was under one ownership or control, any excess in land area over that required to support an average density of 13 persons per acre of gross residential area in any final plan previously recorded may be included. In other words, as each successive final plan is submitted, the overall density of all areas shown on recorded final plans within the proposed RPC District as shown on the master plan shall be recomputed so that the average population density of the developed areas within the recorded sections of the RPC zone shall never at any time in the history of the development exceed a density of 13 persons per acre.

(D) USES PERMISSIBLE

(1) All uses permitted by right or by special permit in any district except RM-3, C-D, CDM, C-G or industrial shall be

permitted in an RPC District. Not more than 1.5 acres per 1,000 persons may be used for uses permissible in the C-N zone. Uses permissible in a C-N zone may be located within the same building as multi-family dwellings provided the C-N uses is on a separate floor or its entrance is on a separate side of the building from the residential entrance. Motels shall also be permitted subject to the provisions contained in the CDM District.

(2) Uses in an RPC District shall be permissible only in the location shown on the approved preliminary plan required by Section 30-68.2(b).

(3) The initial use of any area within an RPC District shall be shown by the plan required in Section 30-68.2(b). Thereafter the use of neighborhood commercial property shall be governed by the uses allowed in the C-N District, the use of all dwelling units shall be governed by the uses allowed in the R-12.5 District, except that no use shall be denied solely because a particular lot has less than the minimum area, less than the minimum setback, less than the minimum frontage, or less than the minimum parking requirements in the C-N or R-12.5 District, provided the minimum parking requirements are met in a different location, as the case may be.

(E) Lot Sizes and Building Location Requirements

The location of all structures shall be as shown on final plans required by Section 30-68.2(b). The proposed location and arrangement of structures shall not be detrimental to existing or prospective adjacent dwellings or to the existing or prospective development of the neighborhood. Open spaces between structures shall be protected where necessary by adequate covenants, running with the land, conveyances or dedications. There shall be no minimum lot size, no minimum setback lines, no maximum percentage of lot coverage and no minimum lot width in an RPC District. However, every single family dwelling shall have access to a public street, court, walkway or other area dedicated to public use and no single family dwelling (except a town house or semi-detached dwelling) and no addition to any single family dwelling shall be erected within a distance of less than 24 feet from any other single family dwelling.

2. Subdivision Open Space Regulations, Baltimore County, Maryland (effective December 10, 1963)

A. Purposes of this section

The purposes of providing for local open space tracts as defined in Sec. 23-1 (ee) of the Baltimore County Code, 1958, are to offer recreational opportunities close to home, to enhance the appearance of neighborhoods through preservation of natural green spaces, to counteract the effects of urban congestion and monotony, and to encourage participation by all age groups in the use and care of local open space tracts in new residential subdivisions. Such types as local parks, small recreation areas, and other small open spaces in a planned neighborhood pattern are intended to conserve local spots of natural beauty, to provide structure to neighborhood design, to add to the sense of spaciousness, to encourage cooperative relationships between neighbors, to help promote the public health, safety, morals and welfare of the people residing nearby, and to aid in stabilizing property values.

B. Designation of local open space tracts in residential subdivisions

No preliminary plan for the proposed development of land for residential purposes in Baltimore County shall be approved by the planning board unless such plan provides for local open space tracts, (as defined in Sec. 23-1 (ee) of the Baltimore County Code, 1958,) of suitable size, location, shape and topography, and with convenient pedestrian access, such tracts to be incorporated in the design of the subdivision through one of the approved methods for applying lot allocation and design standards as set forth in this section, with such exceptions as are hereinafter provided, and contingent upon the adoption of appropriate amendments to the zoning regulations of Baltimore County consistent with the requirements herein.

In the case of apartment developments such appropriate portions of the land as are proposed as open area on the site plan, exclusive of parking areas and driveways, shall be so located and planned as to provide, for apartment residents, local open space amenities of such types as will serve the purposes designated in subsection "A", with openness comparable in quality and character to that of non-apartment subdivisions.

In the case of two or more adjacent subdivisions, developers may cooperatively allocate open space tracts, the coordinated location and design of which shall be subject to planning board approval.

C. Minimum and maximum sizes of such tracts

The area set aside for each local open space tract shall be not less than 20,000 square feet, with the exception of such features as special street center islands other than those normally required as median strips for boulevard-type motorways, and recreational walkways including those that have wider rights of way than are required in the subdivision regulations for normal street sidewalks and block crosswalkways. The maximum area for any separate local open space tract or any considerably enlarged space which is part of an essentially lineal pattern of local open spaces excluding local stream valley parks or green belt buffers, is three acres.

Where practical difficulties or unusual hardship are encountered, a lesser minimum area, or a greater maximum area than the aforegoing may be authorized by the planning board with the written approval of the director of recreation and parks and of the director of public works. If the application of the allocation standards contained in subsection "E" hereof would result in local open space tracts which are too small to be satisfactory, the planning board, upon the recommendation of the board of recreation and parks, may waive the requirement of allocation of local open space tracts as a condition of approval of the preliminary plan of a subdivision. Each preliminary plan submitted by a developer shall clearly show all of the contiguous property holdings of such developer so that the purpose and intent of this section cannot be circumvented; and it shall be the obligation of the planning board to take suitable steps to assure that the developer is not omitting any of his contiguous holdings from said preliminary plan.

D. OWNERSHIP, IMPROVEMENT AND MAINTENANCE OF LOCAL OPEN SPACE TRACTS, WITH THE EXCEPTION OF APARTMENT PROJECTS

Local Open space tracts, at the option of the developer, may be retained permanently by him, or deeded by him to the county. When such tracts are retained by the developer, plans for improvement and maintenance of these tracts must be approved by the board of recreation and parks, and suitable deed covenants made to assure both continuing use of the tracts for local open space purposes and proper operation and maintenance of the same to said board's satisfaction.

As an alternative, the developer, at his option, may deed a local open space tract to the county. The local open space tract shall be suitably managed and maintained primarily for the use of nearby residents. After acceptance by the county of title to such local open space tracts, and if so requested by a local improvement association, the board of recreation and parks may arrange with the association to cooperatively undertake the improvement or maintenance of such tracts, to the extent mutually agreed upon..

Acceptance of a local open space tract, when conveyed by a developer, shall be endorsed upon the deed by the county executive and recorded with the deed such land being properly restricted for use only as local open space, in perpetuity.

Where local open space tracts are to be conveyed to the county in fee, the developer shall convey them at the stage and in the condition agreed upon in connection with processing and approval of the subdivision. Title to the land shall be unencumbered. The county shall take title to such land at a time approved by the director of public works and, in any case, not later than the time at which title to the streets in the subdivision are accepted by the county. It is the intent of this legislation that, prior to acceptance by the county, the developer shall not be compelled to improve the condition of a local open space tract, the original land features of which, within the context of the final and approved development plan, make it suitable as open space. In the case of apartment projects all land shall be retained and maintained by the apartment owner. The county shall share proportionately in the cost of necessary streets, curbs and gutter abutting open space land, execpt in apartment projects.

E. STANDARDS FOR ALLOCATION OF LOCAL OPEN SPACE TRACTS

(1) Percentage allocation. Quantitative minimum standards for allocation of acreage for local open space tracts shall be determined, except as hereinafter noted, as a percentage of the total gross residential acreage of the subdivision. "Gross residential acreage" is the residentially zoned acreage within the perimeter of the subdivision proposed for residential development, plus not more than half the width of existing or recorded boundary streets (maximum 60-foot right of way) to which the subdivision has right of access, except storm drainage reservation strips to the extent that they exceed in area 15 per cent of the subdivision, or waterfront areas below mean low tide. The required local open space allocation schedule applicable to residential zones in the Baltimore County Zoning Regulations (1955) is as follows:

TYPE OF DWELLING UNIT AND ZONE	PER CENT ALLOCATION
R-10 Zone	3
R-6 Zone, One-family	5
R-6 Zone, Two-family	6
R-G Zone, Two-family	8
R-G Zone, Group house	12

In an R-10 Zone the subdivider may elect to set aside local open space tracts in accordance with the cluster method of subdivision as provided for in subsection "F" of these regulations, rather than the method described in this subsection. Regardless of method chosen, in the R-10 Zone not less than three per cent of the gross residential acreage of the tract must be allocated to local open space, except where the development results in a density below the governing low density specified in subsection E(2), in which case the requirements of subsection E(2)(c) shall apply. Coincident with the adoption of appropriate amendments to the zoning regulations, a reduction in minimum permitted lot sizes by not more than five per cent of the minimum required area of any individual lot is allowed.

(2) Densities and area allocations — Densities and area allocations, as hereinafter set forth, shall be applicable along with percentage allocations hereinabove set forth:

DENSITIES AND AREA ALLOCATION STANDARDS

	Gross Residential Density (Gross Residential Acreage Divided into Number of Dwelling Units)			Local Open Space Equivalent, Area Allocation per lot, square feet (Based on maximum permitted density)
	Maximum Permitted Density	Normal Density	Governing Low Density	
R-10	3.2	2.75	2.50	410
R-6 (one-family)	4.5	3.70	3.30	485
R-6 (two-family)	6.00	5.50	5.00	435
R-G (two-family)	6.60	6.00	5.40	530
R-G (Group house	10.50	8.65	7.80	500

(a) when the density of development results in a yield in the range between the maximum density and the governing low density, indicated by zone above, the minimum local open space allocation shall be as required in the table of percentage allocation. If there is a mixture of residential use types, a combination of the local open space standards may be used to yield the total acreage required for local open space tracts.

(b) If the development density yield is between the normal and the governing low, and if no lots are reduced in area below the permitted minimums, and if the developer elects to convey the local open space tracts to the county in fee, the county in connection with the public works agreement shall credit the developer for the acreage difference between the local open space allotment percentage and the local open space yield figured as the number of lots in the proposed subdivision multiplied by the per lot square foot allocation. When a credit is given by the county, such amount shall be based on fair market value.

(c) If the development density yield is below the governing low, the amount of local open space required shall be figured as the number of lots multiplied by the per lot square foot allocation. If the lots of any subdivision meet R-40, R-20, or R-10 standards, regardless of the actual zoning, the cluster method as set forth in subsection F may apply.

F. CLUSTER SUBDIVISIONS AND LOCAL OPEN SPACE TRACTS

When the zoning regulations of Baltimore County shall have been amended to so permit, subdivisions in the R-40, R-20 and R-10 zones may provide one or more areas for local open space tracts through reduction of permitted minimum lot areas and lot widths in accordance with the following schedule, if land at least equal in area to the aggregate amount by which the lots are reduced is designated as local open space in the approved subdivision plan and allocated for joint use by the subdivision residents. Where public or community water and sewer facilities are lacking, the Health Department may stipulate larger lot sizes than indicated below.

	Lot size, Average	square feet Minimum	Max. per cent of lots below average	Min. width for lot below average size
R-40 (Cluster)	30,000	25,000	75	100'
R-20 (Cluster)	16,000	13,000	75	80'
R-10 (Cluster)	8,500	7,500	50	65'

In cluster subdivisions, covenants subject to approval of the Board of Recreation and Parks to insure permanence and proper use of the open space tracts must be recorded. The provisions of sub-section D do not apply to cluster subdivisions.

G. ALLOCATION OF STORM DRAINAGE RESERVATION STRIPS TO LOCAL OPEN SPACE USE

In applying local open space requirements to subdivisions other than cluster subdivisions referred to in subsection "F" where a storm drainage reservation strip is necessary for flood control and if preservation of the natural assets of the land including its vegetation, are provided for in a graphic or written plan subject to approval of the office of planning and zoning, in accordance with the public works agreement, such land may account for 50 per cent of the local open space required. In exceptional cases, where the storm drainage reservation strip(s) satisfies the foregoing requirement, upon approval of the office of planning and zoning, with concurrence of the department of recreation and parks, and depending upon such factors as the appropriate size, degree of park-like character of the storm drainage reservation strip(s) and its location in the subdivision, more than 50 per cent of such strip(s) may be used to satisfy the local open space requirement.

H. DESIGN AND PROCEDURES MANUAL FOR DEVELOPERS

The office of planning and zoning and the department of recreation and parks shall jointly prepare (and from time to time revise) and their respective boards adopt a manual of design and administration of these regulations, such manual to serve as a guide for developers and as an aid in the administration of the provisions of these regulations. Provisions of this manual shall tie into related portions of the public works manual.

3. Community Unit and Density Development Ordinances; St. Louis County, Missouri

1003.270 COMMUNITY UNIT PLAN — 1

The owner or owners of any tract of land comprising an area of not less than twenty acres may submit to the County Council a plan for the use and development of all the tract of land for residential purposes. The development plan shall be referred to the County Planning Commission for study and report and for public hearing. If the Commission approves the development plan, the plan, together with the recommendations of the Commission shall be accompanied by a report stating the reasons for approval of the application and specific evidence and facts showing that the proposed community unit plan meets the following conditions:

(1) That property adjacent to the area included in the plan will not be adversely affected.

(2) That the plan is consistent with the intent and purpose of this Chapter to promote public health, safety, morals and general welfare.

(3) That the buildings shall be used only for single family dwellings, two family dwellings or multiple dwellings and the

al accessory uses as garages, storage space and community
vities, including churches.

(4) That the average lot area per family contained in the
, exclusive of the area occupied by streets, will be not less
n the lot area per family required in the district in which the
elopment is located. If the County Council approves the
n, building permits and certificates of occupancy may be issued
n though the use of the land, the location of the buildings to
erected in the area, and the yards and open spaces contem-
ted by the plan do not conform in all respects to the district
ulations of the district in which it is located. The County
uncil may also authorize the repair or remodeling of any
sting community development that does not conform with the
trict regulations of the district in which it is located. The
unty Council may also authorize the repair or remodeling of
y existing community development that does not conform with
district regulations of this Chapter.

3.285 DENSITY DEVELOPMENT PROCEDURE — 1

The purpose of this section is to provide permissive voluntary
ernate zoning for all single family residential districts except
"E" 6,000 Square Foot Single Family Residential District
d thereby make provisions for variation in lot sizes in said
gle Family Residential Districts by permitting the density of
elling units contemplated by the minimum lot size require-
nts within the various residential Single Family Districts to
maintained on an overall basis when applied to specific tracts
land and thereby provide for desirable and proper open air
ace, tree cover, recreation areas or scenic vistas; all with the
ent of preserving the natural beauty of St. Louis County,
issouri, while at the same time maintaining the necessary
aximum population density limitations of the particular Single
mily Residential Districts.

(2) The developer of a subdivision in any Single Family
strict except the "E" 6,000 Square Foot Single Family District
ne, may, upon receiving the approval of the County Council
his Density Development Plan, vary the lot sizes within a
bdivision from those sizes required by the applicable zoning
strict by compliance with the procedures set forth in this
ction.

The land utilized by public utilities as easements for major
cilities such as electric transmission lines, sewer lines, and
ter mains, where such land is not available to the owner for
velopment because of such easements, shall not be considered
part of the gross acreage in computing the maximum number
lots that may be created under this procedure. The land within
e flood plains of the Missouri, Mississippi, and Meramec Rivers
within the normal banks of other water courses, shall not be
nsidered as part of the gross acreage in computing the maximum
mber of lots that may be created under this Section, unless
e same shall have been reclaimed by proper engineering
ethods.

The maximum number of lots that may be approved shall
e computed by subtracting from the total gross area available
r subdivision under this Density Development Procedure a
xed percentage of said total for street right-of-way purposes
d dividing the remaining area by the minimum lot area re-
uirement of the Single Family District or Districts in which
e subdivision is to be located. The fixed percentages for street

right-of-way purposes to be subtracted from the total area to be
subdivided shall be as follows:

"B"	One Acre Single Family District	15 per cent
"B-1"	30,000 Square Feet Single Family District	15 per cent
"C"	20,000 Square Feet Single Family District	20 per cent
"C-1"	15,000 Square Feet Single Family District	25 per cent
"C-2"	12,000 Square Feet Single Family District	25 per cent
"C-3"	10,000 Square Feet Single Family District	30 per cent
"D"	7,500 Square Feet Single Family District	30 per cent

This method shall apply regardless of the amount of land actually
required for street right-of-way.

3. Under this Density Development Procedure, no lot in a
Single Family Residential District shall be reduced in area below
the following minimum standards:

Zoning District	Required Minimum Lot Area of District	Permissive Minimum Lot Area of Density Development Procedure
"B"	One Acre	20,000 Square Feet
"B-1"	30,000 Square Feet	15,000 Square Feet
"C"	20,000 Square Feet	12,000 Square Feet
"C-1"	15,000 Square Feet	10,000 Square Feet
"C-2"	12,000 Square Feet	9,000 Square Feet
"C-3"	10,000 Square Feet	7,500 Square Feet
"D"	7,500 Square Feet	6,000 Square Feet

Provided further that such reduced lots shall not contain a
frontage less than the applicable frontage required in the subdivision regulations.

4. (a) Under this Section, lots may be reduced in area
below the minimum lot size required, by the Residential District
Zone in which the Subdivision is located, provided that the
average lot size of the total lots created within the subdivision
is not below the minimum lot size required in the applicable
District.

(b) In subdivisions containing ten or more lots, common
land for open space or recreational use may be set aside for
common use by all the owners of the residential lots and such
common land may be included in the total gross acreage used
for determining the average lot size of the total lots created in
such subdivision.

(c) Only the following land uses may be set aside as common
land for open space or recreational use as hereinabove provided
in subsection 4(b):

1. Private recreational facilities, such as golf courses or
swimming pools, which are limited to the use of the
owners or occupants of the lots located within the subdivision.

2. Historic building sites or historical sites, parks and parkway areas, ornamental parks, extensive areas with tree
cover, low land along streams or areas of rough terrain
when such areas are extensive and have natural features
worthy of scenic preservation.

5. Applicants desiring to make use of the voluntary alternate
zoning of the Density Development Procedure as provided by
this section shall file a Petition with the St. Louis County Council
therein setting forth the area and the plan proposed under this
Density Development Procedure together with two true and

correct copies of said petition and plan for the use of the St. Louis County Planning Commission. Before approving any such Petition and plan, which approval shall be by Order of the Council, the County Council shall refer the proposed plan to the County Planning Commission, which Commission shall be given thirty (30) days in which to make a report and recommendation regarding the effect of the application of the proposed Density Development Procedure to the area and subdivision proposed in the Petition. No action shall be taken by the County Council upon any Petition proposing development under this Density Development Procedure until and unless the Report of the Planning Commission is filed, provided however, that if no report is received from the Planning Commission within forty-five (45) days, it shall be conclusively presumed that approval of the Petition has been given by the said Commission and thereafter the County Council shall consider such Petition and plan and shall by its order approve and authorize or deny said Petition and plan.

6. (a) All open space, tree cover, recreational area, scenic vista or other authorized use land, whose acreage shall be utilized in the determination of the common land as is hereinabove provided, shall be conveyed in fee simple title by warranty deed from the Subdivider to Trustees, who shall be provided for by Trust Indenture for each subdivision authorized under this Density Development Procedure, for the sole benefit, use and

enjoyment of the lot owners, present and future, of said su division for a term of years certain, which term shall be for least a period of twenty (20) years, or for the duration of t subdivision, whichever period of time shall be the least, af which period of time fee simple title shall be vested in said owners as tenants in common. The warranty deeds and tr indentures complying with the provisions of this subsection sh have attached thereto a written legal opinion prepared and sign by an attorney licensed to practice law by the State of Missou said opinion shall set forth the attorney's legal opinion as to t legal form and effect of said deeds and indentures. The sa deeds and indentures shall be approved by the Planning Co mission and shall be filed with the Recorder of Deeds of St. Lo County simultaneously with the recording of the final plat of t subdivision authorized under this Section.

(b) The intent and purpose of this subsection 6 is to provi as a condition for the approval of a voluntary alternate zoni density development procedure the requirement, that the lan hereinabove, in the first paragraph of this subsection 6 enum ated as part of the gross acreage, shall be set aside as comm land for the sole benefit, use and enjoyment of the subdivisi lot owners, present and future, for the duration of the speci subdivision or for a period of at least twenty (20) years and further provide that thereafter the said lands shall be held common by said lot owners as tenants in common. (No. 194

4. Planned Unit Development Ordinance; San Francisco, California

Section 304e [as revised February 1962] The authorization of a Planned Unit Development as described herein shall be subject to the following additional conditions. The Planning Commission may authorize the development as submitted or may modify, alter, adjust or amend the plan before authorization, and in authorizing it may prescribe other conditions as provided in (c). The development as authorized shall be subject to all conditions so imposed, and shall be excepted from other provisions of this Code only to the extent specified in the authorization.

I. CATEGORY A

1. The application must be accompanied by an overall development map showing the use or uses, dimension and locations of proposed structures, of parking spaces, and of areas, if any, to be reserved for streets, parks, playgrounds, school sites and other open spaces, with such other pertinent information as may be necessary to a determination that the contemplated arrangement or use makes it desirable to apply regulations and requirements differing from those ordinarily applicable under this Code.

2. The tract or parcel of land involved must be either in one ownership or the subject of an application filed jointly by the owners of all the property included or by the Redevelopment Agency of the City. It must constitute all or part of a Redevelopment Project Area, or if not must either include an area of at least three (3) acres or be bounded on all sides by streets, public

open spaces or the boundary lines of less restrictive use distric

3. The proposed development must be designed to produ an environment of stable and desirable character, and m provide standards of open space and permanently reserved are for off-street parking adequate for the occupancy proposed, a at least equivalent to those required by the terms of this Co for such occupancy in the zoning district. It must include pro sion for recreation areas to meet the needs of the anticipa population or as specified in the Master Plan.

A conditional use of this category may contain, as an integ part of a residential development, a shopping center for servi to the residents, if designed as a unit of limited size and controll by more restrictive and specific regulations than would res from a reclassification of the area so used to a C district. N other commercial use of any Planned Unit Development in a R district shall be authorized except an office building or buil ings to be occupied primarily by administrative, clerical, accou ing or business research organizations, where the principal u does not involve any of the following:

1. The handling or display on the premises of any mercha dise, or the rendering of any merchandising services except permitted as an accessory use for the accommodation of t occupants;

2. Frequent personal visits of clients, members or custome or other persons not employed on the premises;

3. Show windows or exterior display advertising of any kin

I. CATEGORY B

An application for a Planned Unit Development may be filed by a governmental agency in connection with the proposed acquisition of private property for public use, and for the purpose of subsection (a) the governmental agency shall be deemed the owner of the property included in the application whether or not the agency has acquired or proposes to acquire said property. The property included in the application, however, must be the surplus portion of lots acquired or proposed for acquisition for public use or the non-acquired portion of lots only partially acquired or proposed for acquisition for such use. The purpose of a Planned Unit Development of this category is to authorize the Planning Commission to grant exemptions from the requirements of this Code where required by the public interest in order to permit the improvement of said surplus or non-acquired property, and for this purpose the Planning Commission may grant exemptions from the requirements of this Code other than those requirements pertaining to use districts in Article 2. The Planning Commission may grant exemptions as herein authorized:

1. if the general public interest and the interests of the immediate vicinity require that said property be usable for non-public purposes;

2. if the governmental agency submits a plan for the reasonable use of said property in keeping with the objective that the proposed public use cause a minimum disruption of the community and loss of community resources; and,

3. if the requirements normally applicable under this Code would make the preparation of such a plan and achievement of this objective impossible or infeasible.

5. Open Space Covenant, Fremont, California

This form, one of a series worked up by Fremont's planning commission, is used for assuring that a subdivision's open spaces will remain open and not later be filled in with more buildings. It is used for spaces held by the developer or deeded by him to the homeowners; whoever owns the spaces, the city has acquired an interest in them and can enforce their conservation.

COVENANT

(Open Space on Lot ...., Block ...., Tract ....)

WHEREAS, the undersigned ...., hereby warrant that they are the owners of real property in the City of Fremont, County of Alameda, State of California, described as Lot ...., Block ...., of Tract .... That they are in the process of developing said Tract .... with dwelling units and accessory installations and improvements, and

WHEREAS, the City of Fremont, pursuant to Sections 6950 to 6954, inclusive, of the Government Code of the State of California, is empowered to acquire a covenant as to said Lot ...., Block ...., of Tract ...., or an interest therein, so as to limit the future use of and otherwise conserve the open spaces and areas within said land.

Now, THEREFORE, for valuable consideration, the undersigned owners of the real property as herein described hereby individually and jointly, warrant and covenant that all of Lot ...., Block ...., of Tract ...., in the City of Fremont, County of Alameda, State of California, shall be and hereby is dedicated as open space and open area, and no structures or other artificial facilities shall be constructed in or upon said real property without the express consent and authorization of the City Council of the City of Fremont; provided, however, that there shall be reserved to the owner or owners of said real property the right to construct necessary and appropriate structures and facilities for use as a homeowner's park and recreational facility for the benefit of the owners of other parcels in said Tract ...., any such structures and facilities to be subject to the appropriate use permit provisions and procedures as set forth in the Zoning Ordinance and regulations of the City of Fremont and any future amendments thereto, and further subject to final approval by the City Council.

The acceptance of this instrument by the City Council shall not be deemed or construed to waive any other requirement of the Fremont Municipal Code or any other ordinance or regulation in effect in said City.

The warranties and covenants herein contained shall be and remain in effect until all or any thereof are expressly released by the City Council of the City of Fremont, and are intended to be and shall continue to be covenants running with the land hereinabove described and shall be binding upon the legal representatives, successors and assigns of the undersigned.

IN WITNESS WHEREOF, the undersigned have hereunto set their signatures and seals this ....day of.........................., 1962.

APPENDIX D: HOMEOWNERS ASSOCIATION FORMS

1. Articles of Incorporation and Deed Form
Dudley Square, Shreveport, Louisiana

This form covers the key requirements of a homeowners association in language clear enough that a homeowner can understand it — an advantage not always found in such documents. For some reason, however, lawyers' pens get sticky whenever they come to the section saying who's to be in charge and the article about directors is no exception. What such articles provide is that the developers' men will run the outfit until homeowners replace them.

ARTICLE I.   The name of this corporation is DUDLEY SQUARE

ARTICLE II.   Purposes

This corporation is organized for the following purposes and to carry on the following purposes:

(1) To own real estate.

(2) To accept from Dudley Square Development Company, Inc., title to Lot 21 of Dudley Square, being a re-subdivision of Lot 157, and all of Lot "A" of Plot 156, South Highlands Park Addition, Unit No. 2, of the City of Shreveport, Louisiana, to be held in trust for the use and benefit of the owners and occupants of Dudley Square and said property is not be be sold.

(3) To maintain all of the common park area, the brick wall surrounding Dudley Square, the service walks, the paved street, the storage garage, and the street lights located within Dudley Square, and to render all services necessary to assure efficient, attractive and satisfactory maintenance.

(4) To do those acts necessary or proper to accomplish the purposes expressed or implied herein or which may be incidental thereto.

(5) Acting through its Board of Directors, to enter into a contract with an individual or individuals as may be selected by said Board of Directors to perform or accomplish any or all of the purposes of this Corporation, under such terms and conditions and for such compensation as the Board of Directors may consider in the best interest of the Corporation.

ARTICLE III.   Duration

The Corporation shall enjoy corporate existence for a period of ninety-nine (99) years from date hereof.

ARTICLE IV.   Registered Office

The location and post office address of its registered office is: 102 Henry C. Beck Building, Shreveport, Louisiana.

ARTICLE V.   Registered Agents

The full names and post office addresses of its registered agents are: Noah O. Thomas, Jr., 102 Henry C. Beck Building, Shreveport, Louisiana; Harry R. Nelson, 202 Henry C. Beck Building, Shreveport, Louisiana.

ARTICLE VI.   Basis of Organization

(A) This Corporation shall be organized without capital stock and membership shall be evidenced by record ownership in the Conveyance Records of Caddo Parish, Louisiana, indicating ownership of premises in Dudley Square, further identified in Article II herein, and also evidenced by certificate of membership, which certificate of membership shall be in a form approved by the Board of Directors. Membership is limited to twenty (20) in number and restricted to owners of lots in Dudley Square.

(B) Each member shall be entitled to one (1) vote for each home owned in Dudley Square. Ownership of a house in indivision shall constitute only one (1) membership, which membership shall be represented by one (1) individual either by operation of law or by agreement of co-owners.

(C) Membership is transferred by the assignment or sale or by inheritance or testament upon the death of the owner and all rights of membership belonging to the former owner shall inure to the assignee, vendee, heir or legatee of the lot or lots in Dudley Square, as herein identified; and evidence of such transfer of title recorded in the Conveyance Records of Caddo Parish, Louisiana.

(D) In the event of foreclosure sale by a mortgagee and/or Federal Housing Administration as to a lot in Dudley Square, the certificate of membership will be transferred to purchaser at said foreclosure sale. The previous owner will so endorse the transfer of the certificate of membership; however, in the absence of such endorsement by the previous owner, the Secretary of this Corporation is authorized to execute and effect the transfer of said membership.

ARTICLE VII.   Directors

(A) The First Directors are: Noah O. Thomas, Jr.; Thomas B. Tooke, Jr.; Burdette E. Trichel; who shall serve until the election and qualification of their successors.

(B) The direction and administration of this Corporation shall be vested in a Board of Directors composed of three (3) members. Each director shall hold office for a term of one (1) year and thereafter until his successor is duly qualified.

(C) The directors of this Corporation are to be replaced each year at the annual meeting of the members during March f each year by automatic rotation in alphabetical order by the members — that is, commencing with the annual meeting in March of 1960, the three members of the Corporation whose surname begins with a letter or letters which would precede the beginning letter or letters of the surnames of the other members shall replace the three directors named in these Articles of Incorporation, and these three members taking office in March, 1960, would be replaced in that same order at the annual meeting in March, 1961. The Board of Directors will alternate in rotation in this manner.

These provisions pertain only to method of election of directors and do not deprive members of the Corporation of rights granted by law, including right to replace directors at any time notwithstanding his term of office may not have expired; however, directors shall in all instances be elected by rotation as herein provided. In the event of dispute or question concerning capacity of a member to serve as director, the proper person to represent a membership owned in indivision, or the order of rotation of members, the decision of a majority of the members entitled to vote shall be conclusive.

(D) The first officers of this Corporation are as follows: Noah O. Thomas, Jr., President; Thomas B. Tooke, Jr., Vice President; Burdette E. Trichel, Secretary-Treasurer: any two offices of which may be held by one person, except the offices of President and Secretary cannot be held by the same person.

(E) The above named officers shall serve for a period of one (1) year and thereafter until their successors have been duly elected by the Board of Directors and qualified.

(F) Salaries shall not be paid to the officers and/or directors of this Corporation for services as such and dividends shall not be declared.

ARTICLE VIII. Assessments

The Corporation through its Board of Directors may levy regular and/or special assessments to accomplish the purposes of said Corporation which shall be payable to the Treasurer on notice of said assessment.

An assessment shall be assessed against each member in an equal sum of money, and not otherwise.

This provision can be amended only by unanimous consent of the members.

ARTICLE IX. Meetings

(A) At least one meeting shall be held by the voting members each calendar year, which meeting shall take place during the month of March. It shall be the duty of the President, and upon his failure or neglect, then of the Secretary or any officer or member to mail notice at least ten (10) days prior to this Annual Meeting to all members entitled to be present.

(B) Special meetings of the voting members may be called at any time by the President or Board of Directors. On the failure or refusal of either to call a meeting, upon the written request of at least five (5) voting members, any one of these voting members shall have authority to call a meeting, provided that notice by United States mail shall be given to each voting member at least ten (10) days prior to the day named for any meeting called and this requirement of notice shall apply to either regular or special meetings. Meetings may be held at any place within Caddo Parish, Louisiana.

(C) No business transacted at a members' meeting shall be valid unless a quorum is present. A quorum shall consist of a majority of the membership present in person or by proxy.

ARTICLE X. By-Laws

The Board of Directors shall have the power to make, amend and repeal By-Laws to govern this Corporation provided they are in accordance with and do not conflict with these Articles, subject to the power of the members to change their action.

ARTICLE XI. Incorporators

The names and addresses of the incorporators of this Corporation are as follows: Noah O. Thomas, Jr.; Thomas B. Tooke, Jr.; Burdette E. Trichel.

ARTICLE XII. Amendments

The Articles of this Corporation can be amended only by unanimous consent of all members of the Corporation.

EXCERPT FROM DEED TO HOMEOWNER

Lot 1, DUDLEY SQUARE, City of Shreveport, Parish of Caddo, State of Louisiana . . . The premises herein conveyed are located in Dudley Square and subject to easements as set forth in instrument executed by Dudley Square Development Company, Inc., and recorded in the Conveyance Records of Caddo Parish, Louisiana.

Purchaser, by the purchase of these premises herein described, hereby becomes a member of Dudly Square, a non-profit corporation, which holds title to the storage garage and park area shown on recorded plat of Dudley Square. Seller and Purchaser covenant that membership in Dudley Square and ownership of premises herein conveyed cannot be separated — that is, a transfer of title to said premises by operation thereof transfers membership in Dudley Square.

Purchaser, her heirs, successors and assigns, covenants that it will abide by all rules and regulations and pay all assessments which may be imposed by Dudley Square in order to maintain all of the common park area, the brick wall surrounding Dudley Square, the service walks, the paved streets, the storage garage, and the street lights located within Dudley Square, and in order to obtain all services necessary to assure efficient, attractive and satisfactory maintenance, and to pay ad valorem taxes and other operating expenses of Dudley Square.

Purchaser, her heirs, successors and assigns, covenants with each owner, his heirs, successors and assigns, owning other space in Dudley Square, that is firmly bound to maintain premises herein conveyed in good order, clean, good condition and as an attractive residence in Dudley Square, as originally planned and shown on plat of record in Caddo Parish, Louisiana.

Dudley Square Development Company, Inc., its heirs, successors and assigns, hereby declares that any right which is created by reason of the special provisions of this cash sale deed are hereby subordinated to any mortgage executed to finance the purchase, sale or resale of the premises herein described.

2. Kit of Forms for Establishing Homeowners Associations, Hamilton County, Ohio

These forms are part of a package supplied to developers by the county planning commission. They stem from forms drawn up by a developer's attorney for the first subdivision to be planned under the county's community unit plan. With the county's attorney, the planners worked up the final forms, adding a noteworthy provision in the deed giving notice to second owners of their obligations in the maintenance of the common areas.

Honorable Board of County Commissioners
Hamilton County, Ohio
224 Court House
Cincinnati 2, Ohio

Gentlemen:

The undersigned .... owner and developer of a tract of land comprising an area of .... acres in ....Township, known as ....Subdivision, has requested approval to develop it as a Community Unit Plan under article XVI of Section 161, et seq. of the Hamilton County Zoning Resolution.

Recognizing that the Community Unit Plan provisions of the Zoning Resolution permits certain modifications of the normal application of the Zoning Regulations in an area for which a development plan is submitted to and approved by the Board of County Commissioners and further recognizing that the development plan consists of a plot plan and certain written covenants concerning the character of improvements, locations of building lines, grading and the like, we the undersigned, our successors and assigns, owners and developers of the area embraced within the .... Community Unit Plan, do agree to develop said area in accordance with the plan referred to and approved by the Regional Planning Commission following the public hearing on ....1963.

We further agree to insert the following clause in all deeds as a proper notice to second purchasers of the rights and obligations of membership in the .... Community Association:

> "Together with one share of stock of The .... Community Association and all rights and obligations incident to such stock ownership. Provided, however, that no such obligations shall have priority over any mortgage lien now or hereafter effective against these premises and further provided that such rights and obligations are not intended to be construed as covenants running with the land."

We trust that you will be able to approve this plan as a prerequisite for platting the subdivision and issuing zoning certificates.

Respectfully submitted,

ARTICLES OF INCORPORATION
OF
THE .... COMMUNITY ASSOCIATION

The undersigned, all of whom are citizens of the United States, desiring to form a non-profit corporation under the Non-Profit Corporation Law of Ohio, do hereby certify:

FIRST: The name of said corporation shall be The .... Community Association.

SECOND: The place in this state where the principal office of the corporation is to be located is Hamilton County, Ohio.

THIRD: The purpose or purposes for which said corporation is formed are:

(a) To acquire and promote the acquisition of necessary real estate located in .... Township, Hamilton County, Ohio, to be used for park and recreation purposes, which use shall include but not be limited to, playfields, forest areas, picnic and camping areas, swimming pool and other recreation facilities; and to operate and maintain such real estate for park and recreation purposes for the exclusive use and benefit of the residents of the Association.

(b) To convey any part or all of its real estate located in .... Township, Hamilton County, Ohio to township, municipal, county, state or other public authority for public park and recreation purposes, upon the vote of two-thirds of the number of the issued and outstanding shares of the common stock of the corporation at a special meeting of stockholders called and held for the conveyance to public authority as aforesaid; and

(c) To represent and promote the welfare of the residents of .... Subdivision, generally; and to cooperate with the officials of township, municipal, county, state and other public authority for the promotion and betterment of the interests of the residents of said .... Subdivision, including, without limitation, the dedication of drainage ways for the purpose of carrying off storm water or granting easements thereto, to the appropriate township, municipal, county, or state authority requesting said dedication or easement, in any part of the real estate located in............... Subdivision, in order to permit said requesting authority to properly maintain and regulate said drainage ways and easements.

FOURTH: The names and addresses of the persons who are to be the initial trustees of the corporation are as follows:

....

....

IN WITNESS WHEREOF, we have hereunto subscribed our names this..............day of..................., 196   .

AGREEMENT

WHEREAS, The .... Community Association, a non-profit corporation, organized and existing under the laws of Ohio, (hereinafter sometimes called "the Park Corporation"), holds title to a parcel of land comprising .... acres located in .... Township, Hamilton County, Ohio, which said parcel shall be used exclusively for park and recreation purposes in accordance with the restrictions contained in the deed dated ...., 196   , from ...., Grantor, to said The .... Community Association, Grantee, which deed is recorded in Deed Book ...., Page ...., of the Hamilton County, Ohio Records, which said restrictions provide as follows:

> To have and to hold for park and recreation purposes for the exclusive use of the residents of The .... Subdivision, ... Township, Hamilton County, Ohio, (which subdivision is further identified as being that which is shown on a plat recorded in Plat Book ...., Page ...., of the Hamilton County, Ohio Records), upon such terms and conditions as shall be established from time to time by the Board of Trustees of the Grantee (i.e. The .... Community Association) or of the governing bodies of the successors and assigns of the Grantee. Notwithstanding the foregoing, the real estate conveyed hereunder, or any part thereof, may be subsequently conveyed to township, municipal, county, state or other public authority for public park and recreation purposes, not limited to the exclusive use of the residents of .... Subdivision, upon the vote of two-thirds (2/3) of the number of issued and outstanding shares of the common stock of the Grantee, or of the common stock of the corporate successors and assigns of the Grantee, present at a special meeting of the stockholders thereof called and held for the purpose of authorizing the conveyance to public authority as aforesaid.

WHEREAS, the management of the Park Corporation (and thereby, the management and supervision of the use, operation and maintenance of the park and recreation area) shall be vested in a Board of Trustees, consisting of five (5) members (or such other number as may be determined by the stockholders of the Park Corporation in accordance with law); and

WHEREAS, among its other duties, said Board of Trustees shall be responsible for promulgating rules and regulations for the use, operation and maintenance of said park and recreation area, and for raising the funds necessary for defraying the expenses incurred in connection with the operation and maintenance of said park and recreation area, which expenses shall include, by way of example only, real estate taxes, maintenance of grounds, acquisition, maintenance and repair of recreation facilities and legal and accounting services; and

WHEREAS, so long as the park and recreation area is maintained exclusively for the use of the residents of .... Subdivision, it is contemplated that the Park Corporation will have to rely primarily, if not exclusively, on funds raised through the assessment of the residents of said .... Subdivision;

NOW, THEREFORE, in consideration of the conveyance to the undersigned of Lot No ...., Block............ of .... Subdivision, and in consideration of the delivery to the undersigned of one (1) share of the common stock of The .... Community Association, the undersigned, for themselves, their heirs, executors, administrators and assigns hereby covenant and agree with ...., its successors and assigns, and with the said The .... Community Association for their respective use and benefit and of any other person who shall or may become the owner of, or have any title derived immediately or remotely from, though, or under the said ...., its successors and assigns, to any lot situated in .... Subdivision, as follows:

1. So long as the above described park and recreation area is maintained exclusively for the use of residents of .... Subdivision, the undersigned hereby agree to pay, upon presentation of written notice from the Board of Trustees of the Park Corporation, their pro-rata share of the funds required for the operation and maintenance of the park and recreation area, which pro-rata share shall not exceed the sum of $...................per Year. This maximum limitation on the amount of annual assessment can be increased only upon the vote of two-thirds (2/3) of the number of issued and outstanding shares of the common stock of the Park Corporation present at a special meeting of the stockholders thereof called and held for authorizing said increase.

2. The one (1) share of stock of the Park Corporation this day delivered to and accepted by the Grantees, is subject to the restriction that it may be transferred only to the subsequent grantee or grantees of said Lot ...., at the time of such subsequent conveyance.

3. The undersigned further agree to secure an agreement which incorporates the covenants contained in Paragraphs 1 and 2 above from the party or parties to whom any interest in and to said Lot .... is subsequently conveyed by the undersigned.

....

....

3. Homeowners' Association Provisions, Geneva Terrace, San Francisco

These provisions are excerpted from the "Declaration of Restrictions" filed December 17, 1962 by Eichler Homes Inc. The first part, omitted here, contains standard covenants against nuisances, etc, and provisions for an architectural control committee.

PART C.   COMMON AREAS AND PARKING AREAS

C-1. Tract 807, as hereinabove described contains the following lots which are to be referred to hereinafter as "common areas and parking areas," Block 6357, Lot 1; Block 6358, Lot 1; Block 6359, Lots 1 & 2; Block 6360, Lot 1; Block 6361, Lot 1; Block 6362, Lot 1; and Block 6373, Lot 1. The title to said common and parking areas shall be conveyed from Declarant to a non-profit corporate association, which shall be formed by said party upon approval of this Declaration of Restrictions by the City of San Francisco and the Federal Housing Administration. Said conveyances shall be by way of a determinable fee simple vesting title in said Association so long as said property is used and maintained for recreational and parking purposes, on a non-profit basis. Initially, membership certificates in said Association shall be held by Declarant, but upon the sale of Fifty-One per cent (51%) of the properties are sold and occupied by bona fide owners. Thereafter control shall pass to said Association, subject to the terms and conditions herein set forth.

Such Association shall have as its specific purpose, the care, maintenance and utilization of the common and parking areas hereinabove described, for the use, benefit and enjoyment of the members thereof, who shall be the ownrs of residential lots in said subdivision, their successors and/or assigns.

C-2. Said party shall install said common and parking areas, including the improvements thereon, and shall continue to bear the entire cost of maintaining said areas until such time as control shall pass to the Association as above provided. In order to defray the cost of said maintenance, including taxes and insurance, dues at a rate not to exceed ONE HUNDRED DOLLARS ($100.00) per year, shall be levied by said Association upon each member of said Association, and such dues shall be payable on a monthly basis. Declarant agrees to pay the dues for these unsold lots until such time as each lot is sold, at which time the owner shall assume the obligation of his dues. In no event, however, shall Declarant be liable for any dues or cost of maintenance after Fifty-One per cent (51%) of the lots have been sold.

The entire cost of said maintenance shall be borne by said Association. The amount of the annual dues may be decreased by majority action of the Board of Directors of the Association. The maximum dues above provided may be increased by a vote of the majority of the owners attending a meeting called for that purpose.

C-3. In these common areas adjacent to lots that do not face on a street, said common areas shall not contain trees, bushes or other obstructions so as to impede or prevent ready access from the street nearest thereto to said lots. Said open areas shall, however, be cultivated and maintained in a manner similar to the other common areas.

C-4. All residents, and/or property owners, shall utilize the common television and F. M. radio antenna, amplification facilities and underground signal distribution system, as installed and constructed by Declarant, serving each lot, and shall not permit the installation or maintenance of individual television, radio or other antennas, upon any of said lots or residences, without the approval of the Architectural Control Committee.

C-5. Ownership of each lot shall entitle the owner or owners thereof to the use of not more than one automobile parking space, which shall be as near and convenient to said lot as reasonably possible, together with a right to ingress and egress in and upon said parking area. The Association shall permanently assign one vehicular parking space for each dwelling as herein provided.

C-6. Declarant will construct said common and open areas and deliver same to said Association in a fully operable condition. Said common and parking areas, including the improvements thereon, are designed to afford the residents of said subdivision with the maximum of recreational and service facilities. In order to insure that said common and parking areas will continue to be maintained in the high standards set by the builder, the Architectural Control Committee shall have the following powers:

a) If in the opinion of the Architectural Control Committee said common and parking areas are not being maintained in a satisfactory manner, said Committee shall have the right to inform said Board of Directors of said condition and request that it be corrected.

b) Should said Board of Directors refuse to take any corrective action within Fifteen (15) days of being notified by the Architectural Control Committee, said Architectural Control Committee shall have the right to call a general meeting of the members of said Association. This meeting shall take place within Ten (10) days of its call and shall have as its specific purpose a discussion and vote on the specific condition of the common and parking areas as stated by the Architectural Control Committee. The manner and place of said meeting shall be controlled by the by-laws of said organization.

c) Should a majority of all members vote to make the improvements as suggested by the Architectural Control Committee, the Board of Directors of said Association shall be instructed to make said improvements and said Board of Directors shall take immediate steps to comply with said resolution.

C-7. Said Association shall remain in existence so long as its members live in and occupy residences within said subdivision.

C-8. All residents of said subdivision, i.e., holders of title to residential lots therein, shall be members of said Association and shall be entitled to a Certificate of Membership therein. For this purpose, one membership shall be allotted to each residential lot in said subdivision. Upon the sale, transfer, devise, or other conveyance of a lot in said subdivision, the purchaser or purchasers, transferees or devisees thereof shall have transferred to him or them said Certificate of Membership duly endorsed thereon. Certificates are not transferable in gross.

C-9. If the members of said Association or their successors shall fail to pay their dues and/or assessments as the same become due, upon the failure of payments of said dues and/or assessment after Ten (10) days written notice of said delinquency given by said Association to said member, the amount of said dues and/or assessment shall become a lien upon such members's lot in said subdivision in favor of said Association, and said Association shall have the right to record a notice or Claim or Lien and proceed thereon in accordance with the provisions of the California Code of Civil Procedure for the foreclosure and enforcement of liens; or in the event said Association shall not record a Claim or Lien, it shall have the right to commence in action against said member for the collection of said assessment in any court of competent jurisdiction. The enforcement provisions hereof shall be in addition to, and not in derogation of Paragraph D-2 of Part D hereof. All obligations of maintenance, payment of assessments or dues shall survive the determination of the fee and all rights of enforcement shall extend to the holders of the possibility of reverter or their successors in interest.

4. Terrace at Peacock Gap Association

The following are excerpts from the declaration of covenants and restrictions made by the U. S. Plywood Association, the developer. The project is a condominium with an extensive range of services for homeowners, including full maintenance of the exteriors; the articles concerning assessments to pay for all this are notably thorough.

ARTICLE VI.

Powers and Duties: The Terrace at Peacock Gap Association, a non-profit corporation organized under the laws of the State of California, shall have the rights and powers as set forth in its Articles of Incorporation and By-Laws, together with its general powers as a non-profit corporation, and it shall perform each and every duty required of it by this Declaration.

Maintenance: The Association shall maintain the community facilities, the landscape setbacks, the exteriors (including roofs), and the foundations of the residence buildings, and shall engage and pay for all labor and materials as may be reasonably necessary for such maintenance. The Association and such persons as may be engaged by the Association for maintenance purposes, shall have the right to enter upon the exteriors of any residence site for the performance of maintenance but they shall not have the right to enter a residence unit without permission of the Owner of such residence unit.

Operations and Expenses: The Association shall establish such committees as may be provided for in its By-Laws, shall engage a manager, secretaries, engineers, auditors, legal counsel, and other employees or consultants as may be reasonably necessary for the discharge of its duties hereunder. The expenses of committees, the salaries of a manager and other employees, and the fees of consultants shall be established and paid for by the Association. The Association shall pay all other expenses necessary or incidental to the conduct or carrying on of its business.

Enforcement: The Association shall have the duty to enforce each and every of the provisions of this Declaration, including the duty to commence and maintain an action to enjoin any breach or threatened breach of any of the provisions hereof, and to pay all costs of any such action or other enforcement procedure.

Taxes: The Association shall have the authority and duty to pay all taxes and assessments levied against subject property (except taxes levied solely against an individual residence and residence site, which taxes shall be paid for by such owner).

Utilities: The Association shall have the authority and duty to pay the water charges, refuse collection charges, and other charges for utilities required for the common benefit of all owners.

ARTICLE VII.

General Assessment: Each owner shall pay to the Association monthly in advance, on the first day of every calendar month, one-twelfth (1/12) of the annual assessment which shall be established by the Association for the operation of the Association and the operation, maintenance, care and improvement of subject property. Each individual residence and residence site within subject property shall be subject to a lien to secure the payment of the assessment established against it.

Special Assessments: The Association may, from time to time, at a regular meeting or a special meeting called upon notice, establish a special assessment to be levied equally against each residence site for the operation of the Association and the operation, maintenance, care and improvement of subject property. In addition, the Association shall have the authority to establish and fix a special assessment on any residence site to secure the liability of the owner of such residence site to the Association for any breach by such owner of any of the provisions of this Declaration, which breach shall require an expenditure by the Association for repair or remedy. Any special assessment shall become a lien against each individual residence and residence site in the same manner otherwise provided in this Article. Any special assessment shall be payable in full on the first day of the second calendar month next following the date that the same shall be established by the Association.

Collection and Expenditure: The Association shall have the sole authority to collect and enforce the collection of all general and special assessments provided for in this Declaration, and may in addition to such assessments, charge and assess costs (including reasonable attorney fees) and penalties and interest for the late payment or nonpayment thereof. The Association shall have the authority to expend all moneys collected from such assessments, costs, penalties and interest for the payment of expenses and costs in carrying out the duties, rights and powers of the Association and provided for in this Declaration and in the Articles of Incorporation and By-Laws of the Association.

Delinquency: Thirty (30) days after any general or special charge and assessment shall be due and payable, and unpaid or not otherwise satisfied, the same shall be and become delinquent, and shall so continue until the amount of said charge and assessment, together with all costs, penalties and interest as herein provided, have been fully paid or otherwise satisfied.

Notice of Delinquency: At any time after any general or special charge and assessment against any apartment site has become a lien and delinquent, the Association may record a Notice of Delinquency as to such apartment site, which Notice shall state therein the amount of such delinquency and that it is a lien, and the interest, costs (including attorneys' fees) and penalties which have accrued thereon, a description of the apartment site against which the same has been assessed, and the name of the record or reputed record owner thereof, and such notice shall be signed by an officer of the Association. Upon the payment or other satisfaction of said assessments, interest, penalties and costs in connection with which notice has been recorded, the Association shall record a further notice stating the satisfaction and the release of the lien thereof.

Enforcement of Liens: Each lien established pursuant to the provisions of this Declaration by the recording of a Notice of Delinquency as hereinabove provided, may be foreclosed as and in the same manner as is provided for the foreclosure of a mortgage upon real proprety by the laws of California at the date of the commencement of such foreclosure action. In any action to foreclose any such lien the Association shall be entitled to costs, including reasonable attorneys' fees, and such penalties for delinquent charges and assessments as shall have been established by the Association.

Reservation of Liens: Declarant, as to the property covered by this Declaration and each apartment site embraced therein, has established and does hereby establish, reserve and impose a lien thereon securing each assessment provided for by this Declaration, together with said costs, penalties and interest, and Declarant does hereby assign to the Association the right to collect and enforce the collection of the same in accordance with and subject to the limitations contained in each of the provisions of this Declaration.

Subordination to Mortgages: Each and every assessment and lien, together with any costs, penalties or interest, established, reserved or imposed under this Declaration shall be subordinate to any valid bona fide mortgage or trust deed (and the lien and/or title thereof) which has been or may hereafter be given in good faith and for value on any interest of any owner covered by this Declaration. Any subsequent owner of any residence site purchased at foreclosure shall be bound by the restrictions, conditions, covenants, reservations, assessments and liens set out in this Declaration, not including, however, any assessment or lien arising prior to the foreclosure sale.

5. Proposed Charter for The Highlands, Ledyard, Conn.

This is an example of how a homeowners' association can be set up as a special governmental district. Under state law a legal geographical district is set up, the boundaries of which are the same as those of the subdivision. The association has taxing powers and all subsequent buyers of homes have to be members.

SECTION I

All owners of lots, dwellings and other real estate within the limits hereinafter specified in the locality known as The Highlands in the Town of Ledyard, County of New London and State of Connecticut, are constituted a body politic and corporate by the name The Highlands Association.

SECTION II

The limits and territory of said association shall include all lots and land as shown on map # .... on file at the Ledyard Town Hall except for sections A, F, two parcels now owned by Robert O. and Dorothy G. Brown, as designated on said map, and the well sites, as designated on said map.

SECTION III

The territorial limits of said association may be extended at any time so as to include any other land in the Town of Ledyard adjacent to that above described, upon written application of the owner or owners of such other land, in an instrument describing the same and the terms of such proposed annexation, provided such application shall be accepted by two thirds vote of the members present or represented at any annual or special meeting of said association, notice in writing to body, except that adjoining parcels that are developed by Lifetime Homes Incorporated, the Developer shall be incorporated into the Association upon written request without the two thirds vote required hereinabove.

SECTION IV

The purposes for which said association is formed are the following to wit: (See By-Laws)

SECTION V

The Association shall have the power to assess and tax all real property within the territorial limits described herein and added hereto. The current assessment records of the Town of Ledyard shall be used as a basis for determining the amount of assessments on said real property each year. A mill rate shall be selected to meet the budget requirement, but in no event, shall exceed three (3) mills per dollar of assessment, except by 80% vote of the membership.

SECTION VI

All real property owned by the Developer, a utility company, the Town of Ledyard, State of Connecticut, or any agency of the Federal Government shall automatically bear a one hundred (100) percent exemption toward the respective assessments and in turn shall not be entitled to any of the rights and privileges of regular assessed property owners. However, if any such organizations rent or lease property to a tenant, for residential purposes, said property will not carry not carry the exemption during the lease or rental period.

SECTION VII

The Association shall adopt by-laws as drafted and attached hereto, at the first meeting to be held within sixty (60) days from the granting of this Charter. Said meeting shall be held by the Developer whereas every member shall receive, by mail, written notice of said meeting including the purposes of such meeting, which shall include adoption of the by-laws and election of officers.

SECTION VIII

The Board of Governors of the Association shall have the power to enforce compliance to this charter including placing liens upon any property where tax payments are delinquent.

INDEX OF NAMES AND PLACES